NEW YORK STATE AND THE METROPOLITAN PROBLEM

Government Studies

FELS INSTITUTE SERIES
University of Pennsylvania Press

This volume is one of a series devoted to problems of current and long-range significance which are of particular interest to students of local and state government.

Stephen B. Sweeney and Thomas J. Davy (Eds.), *Education for Administrative Careers in Government Service*

Stephen B. Sweeney and George S. Blair (Eds.), *Metropolitan Analysis: Important Elements of Study and Action*

W. H. Brown, Jr. and C. E. Gilbert, *Planning Municipal Investment: A Case Study of Philadelphia*

Reed M. Smith, *State Government in Transition: Reforms of the Leader Administration, 1955-1959*

Harold Herman, *New York State and the Metropolitan Problem*

Oliver P. Williams and Charles R. Adrian, *Four Cities: A Study in Comparative Policy Making*

NEW YORK STATE AND THE METROPOLITAN PROBLEM

by

HAROLD HERMAN

PHILADELPHIA
University of Pennsylvania Press

80807

© 1963 by the Trustees of the University of Pennsylvania

Published in Great Britain, India, and Pakistan
by the Oxford University Press
London, Bombay, and Karachi

Library of Congress Catalog Card Number: 63-7856

Printed in the United States of America

Preface

THIS BOOK is not a description of the metropolitan problem in New York State. Nor is it a survey of the impact of state government upon metropolitan areas. It is an examination of New York's metropolitan policy as derived from and applied to state participation in selected local and joint state-local activities and an evaluation of this policy's impact upon metropolitan integration.

The questions to be asked are: What is New York's metropolitan policy? What is its impact upon metropolitan integration? What is the relative effectiveness of the several tools of intergovernmental relations through which the state influences local compliance with its objectives? And, finally, how much leadership can the state be expected to provide in solving the metropolitan problem?

Because the concept of metropolitan integration is vital to the evaluation that follows, I have felt that a general discussion of the metropolitan problem was warranted in the first chapter. Although the subject has been treated exhaustively and no doubt better by others, I believe the chapter sets a foundation necessary for the rest of the book.

Chapter II reviews New York's expressed attitudes toward metropolitan problems, particularly from the legislative point of view. Chapters III through VI deal with functions chosen to illustrate both the derivation and application of state policy and the alternative methods of state influence in local affairs. Some may believe that other more important functions might have been chosen. Perhaps so, but I feel the generalizations thus derived and discussed in Chapters VII and VIII are applicable to all of the state's dealings with metropolitan areas.

The manuscript was originally prepared in late 1960 and early 1961. Although through later revision I have attempted to bring it reasonably up to date, I doubt if any significant changes in state policy have occurred with regard to either the specific functions here examined, or the metropolitan problem in its entirety, that would seriously modify my conclusions today.

The present publication represents a revision of a dissertation submitted to the Department of Political Science at the Maxwell Graduate School of Syracuse University. The dissertation was begun while I was a Research Fellow in a project examining decision making in the Syracuse metropolitan area sponsored by the Ford Foundation. One of the purposes of the Ford Foundation grant was to provide several graduate students with the opportunity to undertake dissertations in the field of metropolitan study, while participating with senior faculty in the project. The dissertation and its subsequent revision are thus a direct product of that opportunity.

For suggestions, comment, criticisms, and for the intellectual stimulation they provided during our association, I am indebted to the members of the Syracuse project, Profs. Roscoe C. Martin, Guthrie S. Birkhead, Jesse Burkhead, and Frank J. Munger, and then Research Fellows Herbert M. Kagi, Lewis P. Welch, and Clyde J. Wingfield. To Professor Martin a special note of thanks; as project director and dissertation adviser, he added to my already abundant debt to him for years of teaching, encouragement, and guidance.

The present revision was undertaken with the support and encouragement of the Fels Institute of Local and State Government and its director, Prof. Stephen B. Sweeney. I am indebted to him and to my colleagues at the Institute for their help and patience during these past months of rethinking.

During the course of this study and in conjunction with the Syracuse project, many state and local officials and private citizens supplied me with the benefits of their experience in formal interviews and in informal conversation. Their names are too numerous for mention here and to single out a few would fail to express my full gratitude to all. Responsibility for the accurate statement of facts and opinions derived from this source is, of course, solely mine.

A statement expressing appreciation for my wife's help and companionship would necessarily be too lengthy and too personal for inclusion here. My debt to Edith is apparent to all who know her.

HAROLD HERMAN

Philadelphia, 1962

CONTENTS

80807

TABLES AND MAPS

Tables

Maps

NEW YORK STATE AND THE METROPOLITAN PROBLEM

I

The Metropolitan Problem

In 1960, New York's legislature faced what might have been considered an agreeable task of distributing additional aid to local school districts. The distribution was to be a supplement to funds allocated by formula, in effect, a windfall to local districts. Nevertheless, for several weeks, the legislature engaged in a dispute that belied the apparent Republican unity of the state government.

For once, New York City's share of state aid was not a central issue. The dispute took a different form of upstate-downstate conflict, Long Island versus central New York. Leaders of both factions based their appeal for more aid on the problems and needs of metropolitan areas, although the upstaters mercilessly strained the term's application to gain the eventually decisive support of their more rural neighbors.

Regardless of the sincerity, or lack of it, motivating the legislature's reference to metropolitan needs, the mere use of the term is suggestive of the extent to which it has come to dominate state politics. Its use in support of conflicting policies may warrant inferring that the term serves more for purposes of political appeal than preciseness of definition. More to the point, the controversy over educational aid demonstrates that New York's legislative leaders, no less than many others both in and out of public office, seldom agree on the exact meaning of the metropolitan problem and even less often on the means for its solution.

Although the legislature's disagreement may be regarded simply as a not unusual example of sectional bargaining for shares of state aid, no equally simple explanation accounts for differing administrative views of the metropolitan problem. Indeed, administrative officers are as divergent in their approach to the metropolitan problem as legislators. Departmental officers appear to differ in opinion, particularly in regard to state policy toward metropolitan areas, somewhat in relation to the type of agency in which they are located. Members of "staff" agencies are generally critical of state policy, while their "line" colleagues seem more inclined to applaud specific actions stemming from their own respective programs. The latter tend to define the metropolitan problem programmatically, viewing its solution as the individual and collective removal of functional stumbling blocks to effective program performance. The former regard programmatic accomplishments as stopgap, halfhearted measures that fail to attack the heart of THE metropolitan problem.

Academicians disagree as much, if not more, than practitioners. During the several decades academicians have devoted themselves to the metropolitan problem, the diversity of its treatment has grown in proportion to the interest it has attracted. It was to be expected that differences in orientation and interest among the several disciplines now absorbed in the subject would provide varying approaches to the problem. But even among political scientists, whose views are perhaps most relevant to the subject, recent studies have evidenced an increasing variety of methodological and analytical treatments of the metropolitan problem.

Methodological distinctions contribute greatly to political

science's apparent difficulty in intradisciplinary communication. To a generally newer group of scholars, definition of the metropolitan problem hinges upon individual and community perception and behavior and not, as they critically imply, upon the subjective values that underlie their less methodologically inclined colleagues' theories of good government. In their commitment to methodological rigor and to the concept of a neutral descriptive political "science," they offer no suggestions for metropolitan solutions but perform a valuable service in providing techniques for measuring and anticipating public reaction to future proposals.

To the more traditional-minded political scientists, a recognizable metropolitan problem exists, if only due to the failure of political practice to conform with their conceptions of desirable governmental activity. They also accept responsibility for proposing and pursuing measures to improve practice. Identifying the metropolitan problem and posing policy alternatives whereby New York State may contribute to its solution must then concentrate on the works of this latter group, although the former's contributions will serve to introduce feasability and public acceptance as criteria for evaluating the strategic worth of any particular policy alternative. Even thus limited, a definition of the metropolitan problem still leaves considerable room for disagreement.

THE PROBLEM

At its inception, metropolitan study was greatly influenced by the administrative efficiency and governmental reform movements. Structural reorganization was a key tenet of these complimentary movements. Early metropolitan literature, represented by the works of Studenski, Merriam and his colleagues, and Victor Jones, pictured the metropolitan problem primarily as one of structure.[1] After presenting data

---

[1] Paul Studenski, *The Government of Metropolitan Areas,* A Report

indicating the extent of population concentration around large cities, they typically went on to enumerate and describe the many governmental units organized to provide municipal services to these population masses. Service inequalities, a lack of cooperation, and ineffective or non-existent planning for future growth were some of the ills attributed to this complex and irrational governmental pattern. The problem was simple : too many governments. The solution was equally simple : metropolitan government.

True, there were some services that were not as seriously affected by the multiplicity of governments as others. Put another way, governmental activities would not benefit equally when conducted on a metropolitan scale. Nevertheless, all would benefit some. If, as was expected, metropolitan governments could not be created easily or quickly, there were a number of temporary devices that could alleviate the more serious functional manifestations of the problem—water supply, sanitation, traffic, etc. In the final analysis, however, the temporary devices—special districts, annexations, functional consolidations or separations—were merely palliatives and were only preliminary to the establishment of integrated metropolitan governments.[2]

Even in the early years, there were some indications of the intellectual broadening that would accompany later metropolitan studies. Although Merriam, Parratt, and Lepawski hinted that, before they were through, their query would carry them "to a consideration of the basic economic, cultural, and social aspects of urban-rural living, and to a re-examination of the

---

Prepared for the Committee on Metropolitan Problems of the National Municipal League (New York: National Municipal League, 1930); Charles E. Merriam, Spencer D. Parratt, and Albert Lepawsky, *The Government of the Metropolitan Region of Chicago* (Chicago: University of Chicago Press, 1933); Victor Jones, *Metropolitan Government* (Chicago: University of Chicago Press, 1942).

[2] Studenski, *ibid.*, p. 389.

structure and function of American government itself,"[3] a number of years were to pass before political scientists would follow McKenzie's lead and explore the full economic and social implications of the metropolitan phenomenon. To McKenzie, much more than structure and efficiency was involved in metropolitan growth, at stake was the nation's entire economic system, as well as the stability and security deemed essential to wholesome social living.[4]

Perhaps because structural changes failed to accompany the earlier studies or because of the increasing complexity of post-war metropolitan life, scholars soon began to minimize the structural aspects of the metropolitan problem. Fashions in academic terminology, stimulated by foundation funds, encouraged a rash of research and writing tending to place all of life's problems within a metropolitan context. Whereas previous study had dealt with the "fractionated" or "Balkanized" nature of government in metropolitan areas, research itself was "fractionated" in the 1950's, as economic, social, and political problems were singled out for study.

Moreover, the process of research was itself transposed from that of studying problems emanating from the metropolitan complex to that of measuring the impact of the metropolitan area upon specific social, economic, and political interactions.

Ylvisaker has described this type of development as the usual fate of the inquiring mind. "Complications seemed easier to come by than solutions. In the problem of the city one caught hold of the towering questions of life and civilization by the toe."[5] But questions of life and civilization appear to be little

[3] Merriam et al., *op. cit.*, p. 6.

[4] R. D. McKenzie, *The Metropolitan Community* (New York: McGraw-Hill Book Co., 1933), p. 318.

[5] Paul N. Ylvisaker, "Innovation and Evolution: Bridge to the Future Metropolis," *Annals of the American Academy of Political and Social Science,* CCCXIV (November, 1957), p. 158.

affected by governmental structure. The study of organization and structure became outmoded. These became "traditional" subjects of research and as such were kindly, but firmly, put aside.[6]

One resulting redirection of research was an emphasis upon "problems" rather than "the problem" of metropolitan areas. To some, this shift represented a tactical concession to the increasingly mounting political opposition to general governmental reorganization. If some change was to be forthcoming, perhaps it would be necessary to view problems independently, thus encouraging solutions less controversial than total reorganization. To others, however, a more fundamental commitment to existing governmental institutions was involved. They refused to recognize a metropolitan problem but saw rather a number of functional difficulties that could be resolved with but slight modification of the existing system of government. The "crazy quilt" pattern of metropolitan life would eventually right itself in the tugging, hauling, and compromising of a democracy. Time would heal.[7]

Further complications were introduced by those, who, while not content to await resettling of the "crazy quilt," nevertheless expected little to be gained from structural change. It would not accomplish enough, according to Chute, to whom the political problems of a metropolitan area include "but are not dependent upon or limited to, the form of government and the number of units of local government involved." For example, Chute ascribes a number of metropolitan problems to

---

[6] Coleman Woodbury has helped in the reorientation of metropolitan research. He outlines his interests in "Great Cities, Great Problems, Great Possibilities?" *Public Administration Review,* XVIII, No. 4 (Autumn, 1958), pp. 332–340.

[7] Martin Meyerson and Barbara Terrett, "Metropolis Lost, Metropolis Regained," *Annals of the American Academy of Political and Social Science,* CCCXIV (November, 1957), pp. 1–9.

the Island of Oahu, despite the absence there of more than one unit of local government:

[One such] is financial. For example, what public expenditures (or projects) should be undertaken? Who shall pay the bill? . . . To what degree should a metropolitan area spend money on planning and building projects for the long-run future of its area and nearby territory, or, on the other hand, restrict its budget to short-run needs?[8]

What makes the problem Chute describes metropolitan? Is it not a political and budgetary dilemma common to all governments, a problem of policy that is as national and as local in scope as it is metropolitan? If there are any budgetary ramifications of metropolitanism that differ from the universal problem of political choice in allocating resources, are they not necessarily derived from the difficulty of accumulating resources and exercising rational choice through the mechanism of a multitude of governments?[9]

Not only structure but government itself came to be ignored, as political scientists adapted and applied techniques of the sociologists, demographers, social psychologists, and ecologists. The extension of research activity tended to obscure the boundaries of the subject itself. On the one hand, metropolitan problems were completely divorced from governmental considerations. On the other hand, to those political scientists, who retained interest in governmental policy if not organization, the metropolitan problem became indistinguishable from the universal problem of political choice. Is there then nothing

[8] Charlton F. Chute, "The Honolulu Metropolitan Area," *Public Administration Review,* XVIII, No. 1 (Winter, 1958), pp. 8–9.

[9] Although presented to support a view of the metropolitan problem that differs from the orientation of this study, this point is more fully developed by Jesse Burkhead in "Metropolitan Area Budget Structures and Their Implications for Expenditures," Paper read before the 52nd Annual Conference of the National Tax Association, Houston, Texas, October 28, 1959.

unique about the metropolitan problem? Is it merely a question of providing services to large population masses, nothing more than a more obvious and critical form of the general question of American local government: "How can we provide the needed services to everyone at a fair cost and in a democratic fashion?"[10]

Thus defined, however, is the problem solely local? Is not the economic and democratic provision of governmental services a state, national, and international problem as well? The simile begins to strain when extended to the international scene, but it is precisely the similarity of metropolitan and international conditions that challenges this overly generalized concept of the metropolitan problem.

The word *international* connotes the difficulty of achieving an equitable and democratic distribution of world resources. The political boundaries that mark the jurisdictional limits of sovereign nation-states create artificial (albeit self-imposed) distinctions of need and resources. Similarly, the diversity of governments within metropolitan areas deprives its residents of the ability to air and satisfy whatever few or many demands are common to them. If the general problem of local government is *how* to provide services, the problem of metropolitan areas is *who* is to provide services. It is the concentration of population in numerous independent, proximate governmental units that distinguishes metropolitan from local problems.

Whether represented by one or any number of governments, metropolitan, as well as urban and rural, residents will always be faced with the question of how to provide services and with the choice of spending for short or long-run objectives. These are questions of policy—the how's, not the who's. It is within this context that Banfield and Grodzins feel compelled to

[10] Guthrie S. Birkhead, *The Metropolitan Problem* (New York: National Municipal League, 1953), p. 8.

comment on the frequent failure to distinguish between "problems which exist in metropolitan areas" and "problems which exist by virtue of the inadequacies of governmental structures in the metropolitan areas."[11] Hardly necessary twenty years ago, this admonition today contributes a needed element of clarity to the ever expanding range of metropolitan area studies.

The distinguishing political characteristic of a metropolitan area is, by definition, its multiplicity of local governmental units. Ascribing to this one characteristic all of the problems which exist in metropolitan areas is as unrealistic as ignoring it as a source of metropolitan ills. The extent to which government and its structure enter into metropolitan analyses depend upon the observer's choice of the questions of life and civilization to be examined. If the current emphasis on the broad social and economic consequences of urbanism, as evidenced by concern for economic development, racial harmony, or taxpayer reluctance to divert resources from the private to the public sector is to continue, then governmental structure and indeed government itself may necessarily be of only secondary importance. If the question to be examined is less ambitiously defined, government may once again occupy a central role in metropolitan study.

The metropolitan problem is here conceived as the dysfunctional effect that numerous proximate yet independent units of local government impose upon the development and fulfillment of public policy in areas of concentrated population. The effect of an overabundance of governments is to deprive an interdependent population of a forum and market place in which political negotiation and compromise can take place. The irony of local government is such that, by insuring the continued

---

[11] Edward C. Banfield and Morton Grodzins, *Government and Housing in Metropolitan Areas* (New York: McGraw-Hill Book Co., 1958), p. 32.

absence of such political institutions, resistance to consolidation at the metropolitan level serves increasingly to foster centralization at the more removed state and federal levels of government.

THE SOLUTION

To the political scientists who first examined the problem, metropolitan government was the solution. Within the limits of their institutional and primarily administrative orientation, their logic was unassailable, for by definition an area-wide government would eliminate the problem.

The most serious challenge to the political scientists' position questioned the limits they had set to the metropolitan problem. Even on their own terms, however, the advocates of metropolitan government were still not unrefuted. The apparent simplicity of their solution ignored the difficulty of drawing the boundaries of the metropolitan community. Its limits varied for purposes of sewage disposal, traffic control, and every other governmental activity.

A more fundamental criticism questioned the existence of evidence to support the commitment to administrative efficiency, so essential to the integrationists' position. Are not the repeated defeat of proposals for governmental integration evidence, in fact, that administrative efficiency and organizational neatness are hardly capable of inspiring changes in political sentiments and preferences? Moreover, accepting the primacy of efficiency as a goal, one could well demonstrate that consolidation and integration are not necessarily productive of economies of scale.[12]

Integrationists countered by offering a more sophisticated rationale and plan for metropolitan government. To meet

[12] For example: Werner Z. Hirsch, "Expenditure Implications of Metropolitan Growth," *Review of Economics and Statistics,* XLI, No. 3 (August, 1959), pp. 232–241).

objections that an area-wide government would be inflexible, they suggested a pattern of local relations modeled after the federal system. As in the national system, local federalism would be adaptable to changing conditions. There would be no need for detailed initial distributions of functions between the metropolitan and subsidiary governments. The system would develop in time. However, the creation of an area-wide government with general powers was necessary to provide the system with leadership and continuity.

With use of the standard of efficiency declining, a new dimension was added to support metropolitan government. At the same time, it provided a basis for criticizing the continued use of temporary *ad hoc* devices. Governmental integration was no longer advocated merely on administrative grounds; it had social and political value as well. Metropolitan government was the only democratic means of balancing area needs. Furthermore, it would help promote the consciousness of community interest so vital to the future of the area. Thus Robert Wood, who seems torn between the logically persuasive arguments of integration and the sentimental, perhaps irrational, values of diversity and decentralization, hesitantly concludes that metropolitan government must be supported, for

> [The] conditions of urbanity are the basic reasons for supporting the idea of a single metropolitan government, and they seem more logically persuasive than the customary arguments of efficiency and administrative tidiness. A [metropolitan government] is likely not only to be better managed in the professional sense, but more democratically managed as well. . . . By making the metropolis a true political entity, a different type of blending of urban and suburban becomes possible.[13]

Although Wood is inclined to sacrifice diversity to newer

[13] Robert C. Wood, *Suburbia: Its People and Their Politics* (Boston: Houghton Mifflin Co., 1959), pp. 297–298.

values appearing in our society, as was McKenzie earlier, some political scientists and apparently most metropolitan residents prefer that the sacrifice should be made gradually, if at all. Whether motivated by conviction or a sense of strategy, people of this mind usually offer one of two functional alternatives to general governmental integration. One alternative relies upon the use of *ad hoc* devices for piecemeal solutions to specific functional problems. It recognizes, for certain purposes, the inherent inadequacy of the present system of local government in metropolitan areas but stops short of recommending over-all revision of the structure or responsibilities of local governments. The second approach differs in that it seeks to promote adjustments with no structural change at all. Voluntary cooperation and the strengthening of existing units of government are its tools.[14]

The conflict between the New York State Equalization Board and the State Tax Commission illustrates a practical application of the difference in functional approaches. Both organizations are concerned with achieving more equitable local real-estate assessments. The Tax Commission believes a complete revision of the present decentralized system is required. The Equalization Board feels that satisfactory results can be obtained by strengthening local boards and stimulating them to cooperate with one another.[15]

---

[14]A summary of the many approaches to metropolitan study is contained in George S. Blair, "Approaches to Metropolitan Area Study," *Metropolitan Analysis,* eds. Stephen B. Sweeney and George S. Blair (Philadelphia: University of Pennsylvania Press, 1958), pp. 30–44. In particular, pp. 31–37 contrast the functional and integrational views. Blair places those favoring cooperation in the integration camp. Because their efforts are, in practice, directed at specific functional problems and because they differ with integrationists on the need for general area-wide government, this group has been categorized here as a branch of functionalism.

[15]*See* the report of the State of New York, Temporary Commission on the Revision and Simplification of the Constitution, "Real Property Assessments," Staff Report No. 27 (mimeographed, n.d.).

A metropolitan solution that has won increasing acceptance in recent years is one that virtually defies classification. The oft-reported proposal to elevate county government to a prominent role in local affairs has gained added vitality in association with both integrationist and functionalist efforts to solve the metropolitan problem. The urban county[16] often represents an effective (and realistic) compromise between efforts to reorganize local government and desires to retain complete local independence.

Although integrationists point to the many metropolitan areas that now extend beyond the limits of single counties and to their inevitable increase in number, they are grateful for the immediate centralization that can be achieved under county auspices and for the promise that the break-through in county government holds out in the continued battle against decentralization.

The urban-county concept is acceptable to most functionalists too. The county is a traditional, if not everywhere fully operative, unit of government. It can be used as a means of dealing with those special problems that are too great to be handled by local units individually or collectively. The proponents of metropolitan action through cooperation only, however, have good reason to be suspicious of the foothold in centralization thus gained. Assurances that the assignment or withholding of specific functions to counties allows enough flexibility for the protection of local interests is not always enough to overcome their objections to a strengthened county.

In the final analysis, a revitalized county government offers a lesser threat to the traditional concepts of local government

[16] The urban county in this sense refers not merely to a county characterized as urban in population but also to one that is politically and organizationally equipped to provide urban services. *See* Victor Jones, "Federated Forms of Metropolitan Government," *The Future of Cities and Urban Redevelopment,* ed. Coleman Woodbury (Chicago: University of Chicago Press, 1953), p. 591 ff.

and home rule than some of the more drastic proposals for metropolitan government. At the same time, it mitigates some of the more obvious problems stemming from metropolitan growth and serves as a focal point for further reorganization. The urban county thus has some basis of appeal to all groups.

However, a revitalized county that does not assume most, if not all, municipal functions falls far short of the integrationist's goal. Although early proponents of metropolitan government were criticized for overemphasizing institutional and administrative aspects of government and politics, integration today is supported on grounds other than mere efficiency. If, as Wood suggests and as is here defined, the metropolitan problem is that of facilitating the development of needed area-wide policy, its solution demands institutional expression. The integrationist no longer assumes that the mere existence of one government will relieve all the problems *in* a metropolitan area, but he does believe that the presence of the institution can itself promote the consciousness of community need and purpose necessary to elicit and rationally weigh alternative policies.

In effect, the absence of metropolitan consciousness, the factor that influences many to resign themselves to a functional approach to the metropolitan problem, reinforces the integrationist's belief in the immediate need of metropolitan government. Where the functionalist differentiates between governmental and community integration, holding the former dependent upon the latter, the integrationist, alluding specifically to American National experience, asserts that governmental institutions need not result from, but may lead in, the development of a political community. To him, metropolitan government is more than a future probability, it is an immediate necessity.[17]

---

[17] This position is illustrated by two slightly different treatments of the

What of the converse point of view: is political integration dependent upon the existence of institutional integration? In the functionalist camp are many who believe, to the contrary, that gradual stimulation of attachments to a metropolitan community through experience with functional metropolitan solutions is the only solid foundation upon which to build permanent integrated institutions, to which the integrationist replies by characterizing functional action as actually disintegrative and as serving only to insulate the community from the more basic structural governmental problem of the metropolitan area.

At one time, integrationists conceded some value to individual functional improvements in governing metropolitan areas. Criticisms were generally directed at their inability to provide more than temporary relief and their failure to attack the problem comprehensively. Today, there is a tendency to reject even so innocuous a functional device as interlocal cooperation, on the grounds that it both "delays the eventual day of reckoning" and promises to strengthen and thus help maintain the present decentralized pattern of local government.[18] In this view, functional solutions are at best temporary palliatives, at worst deliberately evasive tactics. This strong a commitment to structural reorganization appears to confuse means with ends and to prefer a whole loaf to nothing at all.

This present study is undertaken with a bias toward the integrationist conception of the metropolitan problem but not

---

relationship between community and governmental integration. Drawing heavily on Bogue, Carl F. Kraenzel stresses the role of government as a creator of community in "The Social Consequences of River Basin Development," *Law and Contemporary Problems,* XXII, No. 2 (Spring, 1957), pp. 222–223. Jefferson B. Fordham depicts a somewhat less causative relationship in *A Larger Concept of Community* (Baton Rouge: Louisiana State University Press, 1956).

[18] Blair, "Approaches to Metropolitan Area Study," *op. cit.,* p. 38

80807

with a belief in the overriding necessity of metropolitan government. Metropolitan integration is here defined as both an end and a means. To the extent that governmental integration contributes to the growth of community cohesiveness, it is, at some points in time, less an institutional expression of metropolitan consciousness than a factor in its evolution. But the effort expended in creating and maintaining governmental institutions is itself dependent upon reaching minimal concensus regarding the merits of area-wide treatment of specific governmental functions. Piecemeal functional solutions may indeed reduce the urgency attending the need for governmental integration, but they may also be the most effective means of structuring the minimal concensus required to even approach comprehensive metropolitan reorganization. Public and official familiarity with metropolitan action in an increasing number of functional forms may be a decisive contribution to reducing resistance to more thorough plans for metropolitan government.[19]

Additional considerations also militate against too hastily dismissing the functional approach. Realism is one. A second is the possibility that the tangible results of functional solutions deserve greater weight than their eventual impact upon government in metropolitan areas. One need not be committed to viewing the metropolitan problem as solely a collection of specific functional difficulties to recognize the value of easing transportation or abating pollution in metropolitan areas, despite the resulting delay to the day of reckoning. While

[19] Robert C. Wood characteristically hedges in suggesting that "the solution most scorned by some experts, the 'stop-gap,' ad hoc improvisations . . . [may serve to] bring together different groups of participants to debate and compromise . . . providing at least a basis for the exercise of power under democratic control." "A Division of Powers in Metropolitan Areas," *Area and Power*, ed. Arthur Maass (Glencoe, Illinois: The Free Press, 1959), p. 67. In contrast, *see* his somewhat different evaluation in *Suburbia, op. cit.*, especially p. 13.

governmental integration may be the most desirable path to pursue, it is unpardonable to sacrifice the possible benefits of functional solutions in order to allow problems to multiply to the point where governmental re-organization becomes imperative. Building a new structure upon old ruins may often be less expensive than remodeling, but the social costs of allowing local governments to fall into ruin are much too high.

Thus, an evaluation of New York State's metropolitan policy can be based neither solely upon its effect on governmental consolidation nor exclusively upon its contribution to the alleviation of functional problems. The criteria for measuring the impact of state policy must be generally defined, subject to considerations of "the long run." State policy is here judged integrative, if, in the long run, it contributes to the development or strengthening of:

1. Public awareness of the areal implications of local activities;
2. Popular desire to approach the solution of areal problems on a metropolitan scale;
3. Institutional mechanisms for evoking and organizing public participation in areal policy making.

THE STATES AND THE PROBLEM

Concern with the metropolitan problem has renewed interest in state-local relations. Municipalities are, after all, creatures of the state. General recognition of state influence in metropolitan affairs has not, however, been accompanied by agreement as to its consequences. Most observers trace at least part of the blame for the mess our cities are in to inept, if not malicious, state policy. Others, looking more to the future than the past, foresee the possibility of state leadership contributing significantly to the lessening, if not the eventual solution, of metropolitan problems.

New York State's experience with metropolitan problems offers an excellent opportunity to analyze the possible impact of future state metropolitan policies throughout the country. New York's reaction to metropolitan growth has, of necessity, been more pronounced than that of most states. It has developed a complex pattern of relationships with local governments that embodies sometimes inadvertent, but more often conscious metropolitan policies. The impact of these has been substantial and would in itself justify examination. Furthermore, recent indications suggest that New York's future policy will follow paths already broken. Moreover, other states, if they have not already done so, seem likely to pursue similar paths.

What can states do to help solve the metropolitan problem? The question has been considered in most metropolitan studies or surveys. Suggestions for state action usually present variations on recommendations contained in a report prepared for the Council of State Governments by John C. Bollens in 1956. That document, *The States and the Metropolitan Problem,*[20] still represents the most comprehensive treatment of this aspect of state-local relations.

The States and the Metropolitan Problem can be classified definitely as integrationist. Although it attributed functional components to the general problem and suggested that state governments consider and provide for the use of various functional devices to alleviate the severity of their effects, the report emphasized that the major long-run problem of metropolitan areas is that of inadequate governmental organization. It called upon states to

[establish] general governmental jurisdictions of metropolitan

---

[20] John C. Bollens, *The States and the Metropolitan Problem* (Chicago: The Council of State Governments, 1956).

scope—jurisdictions that are representative of the people directly affected and are accountable and responsive to them.[21]

A most remarkable aspect of the Council's report was the primary role and responsibility it ascribed to states. It suggested that, while appropriate national and local action was indispensable, states held the key to the metropolitan solution. Its recommendations, however, hardly substantiated placement of the key. If anything, they stressed the primacy of local action. Only one recommendation called upon states for anything but advisory or permissive action. In sweeping language, that recommendation suggested that states appraise the adequacy of local governments, making "necessary changes in accordance with the results of the appraisal."[22] The scope of those changes and how they were to be put into effect were nowhere detailed.

Whether primary or secondary, there is no doubt that states have a role to play in metropolitan integration. The Council's report tended to define that role almost exclusively in terms of constitutional and legislative contributions to revisions in local governmental structures and territorial boundaries. In contrast, it is here assumed that states possess a variety of mechanisms, ranging from constitutional and legislative mandate to administrative consultation and advice, through which influence may be brought to bear on local governments. A state's metropolitan policy is thus a reflection of the totality of state-local interactions.

The chapter immediately to follow reviews the development of New York's legislative understanding of the metropolitan problem and the current legislative attitude toward participation in its solution. This understanding has been expressed largely functionally. If the metropolitan problem can be solved only through general governmental reorganization and integra-

---

[21] *Ibid.*, p. 22.
[22] *Ibid.*, p. 132.

tion, then New Yorkers, at least, must look to other sources of leadership than their state government. But the potential impact of state leadership assumes more significant proportions if one accepts the possibility that the path to metropolitan integration may lead through functional solutions. Consequently, subsequent chapters review the state's legislative and administrative participation in four areas of local activity customarily identified with the metropolitan problem: public health; water pollution control; public education; and highways.

Analysis of state activity in each of the functional areas will be concerned primarily with their impact upon metropolitan integration. A complimentary objective is to weigh the relative effectiveness of alternative methods of state participation in local affairs. The actual programmatic results of state policies will be examined only in passing.

A related consideration is the extent to which states should strive for leadership in metropolitan integration. The Council of State Governments obviously believes they should and must. Others are equally convinced that the major responsibility for adjustment, change, reorganization, or whatever will lead to metropolitan integration rests with local governments. To them, the state's duty lies in merely removing obstacles to the exercise of local initiative.[23] Justification of either position, in turn, involves a fundamental question yet to be examined. To what extent are state governments capable of providing leadership for metropolitan integration?

[23] A balanced discussion of the role of the state and local governments, containing an evaluation of both positions, is to be found in Wilfred D. Webb, "Federal, State, and Local Responsibilities in Solving Metropolitan Problems," *Proceedings of the Texas Conference on Metropolitan Problems, May 16–17, 1958* (The University of Texas: Institute of Public Affairs, 1958), pp 64–70.

II

The Legislature's View

New York City has recently been elevated to a supermetropolitan category in Census Bureau listings. Its demographic uniqueness, coupled with the singular treatment it receives from the state, virtually necessitates a decision that might otherwise have been made on the grounds of expediency. As an entity, the New York metropolitan area will not be considered here, although occasional reference will be made to the city and its suburbs.

There are then six urban centers in upstate New York that qualify as Standard Metropolitan Statistical Areas by Census Bureau definition. They vary greatly in geographic and population size and political complexity. The Buffalo S.M.S.A. includes more than $1\frac{1}{4}$ million inhabitants. Erie County's portion has more than 1 million residents distributed almost equally between the City of Buffalo and the rest of the county. The population of the Utica-Rome S.M.S.A. numbers 338,000. Of these, 66,000 are located in Herkimer County, one of the largest in area in the state, and one which contains a good portion of the state's forest preserve.

If a metropolitan area is typified by developing urban conditions, it is well to remember that not all the communities

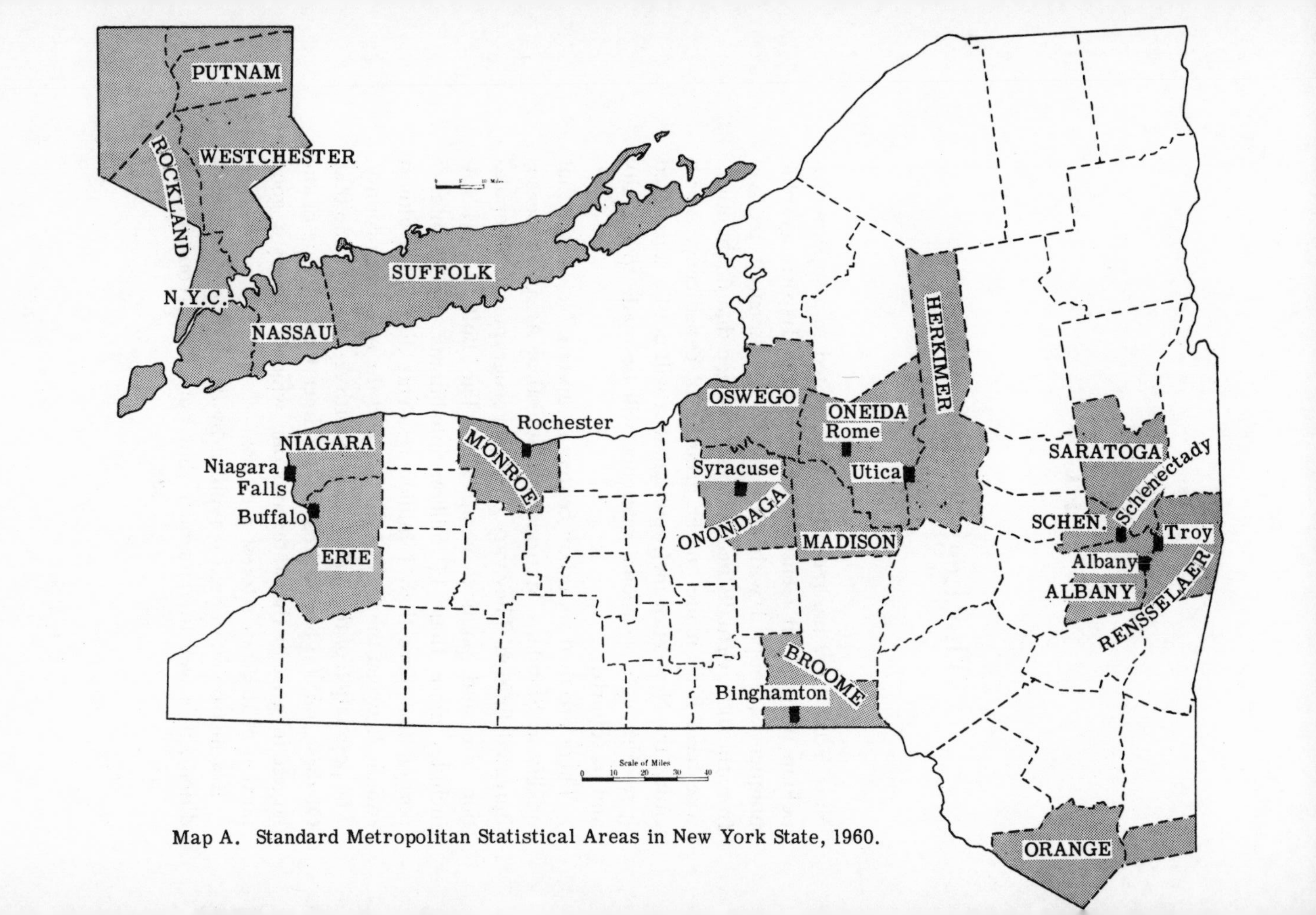

Map A. Standard Metropolitan Statistical Areas in New York State, 1960.

included in the Census Bureau's metropolitan tally are so affected. Even relatively urban Erie County manages to escape full involvement in the problems of urbanization. The County is composed of fourty-four primary units of government—the county, three cities, fifteen villages, and twenty-five towns. As late as 1958, it was judged that ten of these jurisdictions had been relatively unaffected by metropolitan growth and eight others had felt the pressures of urbanization only slightly.[1]

The Census Bureau's use of whole counties for purposes of data compilation seriously dilutes distinctions of complexity both within and between metropolitan areas. Inclusion of all of Herkimer in the Utica-Rome S.M.S.A. is misleading, as well as unrealistic. So too were the recent additions of Madison and Oswego Counties to the Syracuse Area and Saratoga County to the Albany-Schenectady-Troy S.M.S.A.

Some of the misleading connotations of whole-county data were reduced when the Census Bureau injected *Statistical* into the previous title, Standard Metropolitan Area. As Table 2 indicates, identification of the urbanized segments of S.M.S.A.'s also helps dispel the illusion of total urbanity ordinarily attached to the metropolitan label. Nevertheless, as the continued addition of new units and the repeated documentation of population growth in metropolitan areas attest, those areas are normally thought to coincide with county boundaries.

The lack of a clear definition of a metropolitan area other than a statistical one compounds the difficulty of conceptualizing metropolitan area problems and creating instruments for their solution. The task of determining the limits of any one metropolitan area for the purpose of providing governmental services is equally as important (and difficult) as that of defining

---

[1] State of New York, Temporary Commission on the Revision and Simplification of the Constitution, "Metropolitan Buffalo and Niagara Falls," Staff Report No. 25 (mimeographed, December, 1958), pp. 9–11.

Table 1. Population of Central Cities and Outside Areas in the Standard Metropolitan Statistical Areas of Upstate New York 1940–1960

	Area sq. miles	1940 Popula- tion	1940 Per cent	1950 Popula- tion	1950 Per cent	1960 Popula- tion	1960 Per cent	1960 Den- sity	Increase or Decrease 1940–60
ALBANY-SCHENECTADY-TROY									
Albany County									
Albany	19.0	130,577	59.0	134,955	56.4	129,726	47.3	6,828	−0.6
Outside ...	512.0	90,738	41.0	104,391	33.6	143,200	52.7	280	57.8
Schenectady County									
Schenectady ...	10.2	87,549	71.5	91,785	64.4	81,682	53.4	8.008	−6.7
Outside ...	198.2	34,945	28.5	50,712	35.6	71,214	46.6	359	103.8
Renesselaer County									
Troy	9.3	70,304	67.9	72,311	54.5	67,492	47.3	7,257	−4.0
Outside ...	655.7	51,081	32.1	60,296	45.5	75,093	52.7	145	47.0
Saratoga County ...	814.0	65,606	100.0	74,869	100.0	89,096	100.0	109	38.9
Total central cities .	38.5	288,430	54.3	299,091	50.8	278,900	42.4	7,244	−3.3
Total outside ...	2,180.5	242,819	45.7	290,268	49.2	378,603	57.6	174	55.9
BINGHAMTON									
Broome County									
Binghamton ...	10.1	78,309	47.2	80,674	43.7	75,941	35.7	7,519	−3.1
Outside ...	899.9	87,440	52.8	104,024	56.3	136,720	64.3	152	56.3
BUFFALO-NIAGARA FALLS									
Erie County									
Buffalo ...	39.4	575,901	72.1	580,132	64.5	532,759	50.1	13,521	−7.5
Outside ...	1,014.6	222,476	37.9	319,106	35.5	531,929	49.9	524	139.1

Niagara County									
Niagara Falls ...	12.7	78,029	48.7	90,872	47.8	102,394	42.2	8,062	31.2
Outside ...	520.3	82,081	51.3	99,120	52.2	139,875	57.8	269	70.4
Total central cities .	52.1	653,930	68.2	671,004	61.6	635,153	48.6	12,191	−2.9
Total outside ...	1,534.9	304,557	31.8	418,226	38.4	671,804	51.4	438	120.5
ROCHESTER									
Monroe County									
Rochester ...	36.0	324,975	74.2	332,488	61.6	318,611	54.3	8,850	−1.9
Outside ...	637.0	113,255	25.8	155,144	38.4	267,776	45.7	420	136.4
SYRACUSE									
Onondaga County									
Syracuse ...	25.3	205,967	69.8	220,583	64.6	216,038	51.0	8,539	4.9
Outside ...	766.7	89,141	30.2	121,136	35.4	206,990	49.0	270	132.2
Madison County ...	661.0	39,598	100.0	46,214	100.0	54,635	100.0	83	38.0
Oswego County ...	968.0	71,275	100.0	77,181	100.0	86,118	100.0	89	20.8
Total central cities .	25.3	205,967	50.7	220,583	47.4	216,038	38.3	8,539	4.9
Total outside ...	2,395.7	200,014	49.3	244,531	52.6	347,743	61.7	145	73.9
UTICA-ROME									
Oneida County									
Utica	15.8	100,518	49.4	101,531	45.6	100,410	38.0	6,355	−0.1
Rome	77.1	34,214	16.8	41,682	18.7	51,646	19.5	670	50.9
Outside ...	1,134.1	68,904	33.8	79,642	35.7	112,345	42.5	99	63.0
Herkimer County ...	1,442.0	59,527	100.0	61,407	100.0	66,370	100.0	46	11.5
Total central cities .	92.9	134,732	51.2	143,213	50.4	152,056	45.9	1,637	12.8
Total outside ...	2,576.1	128,431	48.8	141,049	49.6	178,715	54.1	69	39.2
THIRTEEN COUNTIES									
Total central cities .	254.9	1,686,343	61.0	1,747,053	56.4	1,676,699	45.8	6,578	−.6
Total outside ...	10,224.1	1,076,516	39.0	1,353,242	43.6	1,981,361	54.2	194	84.1

SOURCE: U.S. Bureau of Census, *Census of Population.*

Table 2. Population of S.M.S.A.'s Residing in Urbanized Areas, 1960

	Total population	Central city	Outside	Urbanized outside	Per cent outside urbanized	Per cent total population urbanized
ALBANY-SCHENECTADY-TROY						
Albany ...	342,926	129,726	143,200	98,274	68.6	66.5
Schenectady .	152,896	81,682	71,214	50,494	70.9	86,4
Rensselaer ...	142,585	67,492	75,093	20,632	27.5	61.8
Saratoga ...	89,096	—	89,096	7,137	8.0	8.0
Total S.M.S.A.	657,503	278,900	378,603	176,537	46.6	69.3
BINGHAMTON						
Broome ...	212,661	75,941	136,720	82,200	60.1	60.1
BUFFALO-NIAGARA FALLS						
Erie ...	1,064,688	532,759	531,929	368,838	69.3	84.7
Niagara ...	242,269	102,394	139,875	50,379	36.0	63.1
Total S.M.S.A.	1,306,957	635,153	671,804	419,217	62.4	80.7
ROCHESTER						
Monroe ...	586,387	318,611	267,776	174,791	65.3	65.3
SYRACUSE						
Onondaga ...	423,028	216,038	206,990	117,248	56.6	78.8
Madison ...	54,635	—	54,635	—	0.0	0.0
Oswego ...	86,118	—	86,118	—	0.0	0.0
Total S.M.S.A.	563,781	216,038	347,743	117,248	33.7	59.1
UTICA-ROME						
Oneida ...	264,401	152,056	112,345	35,257	31.4	70.8
Herkimer ...	66,370	—	66,370	466	0.7	0.7
Total S.M.S.A.	330,771	152,056	178,715	35,723	20.0	56.8
All S.M.S.A.'s .	3,657,700	1,676,699	1,981,361	1,005,716	50.8	73.3

the area for purposes of comparison. The metropolitan community for the purposes of one governmental function frequently fails to coincide with the service area to which others should or do extend. Almost all of Onondaga County is today concerned with the problem of water supply. Highway construction, transportation policies, and traffic control are of importance to only selected communities within the county and interest residents of Madison and Oswego Counties only slightly; and transportation is usually regarded as the most recognizable and popular of metropolitan problems.

The difficulty in defining the metropolitan area is of more than academic concern. It is itself a reflection of the tenuous metropolitan consciousness attached to the specific functional problems that occasionally attract public attention. It is easier to feel part of an area experiencing a recognizable problem of water supply or sewage disposal than to identify oneself with the vague concept of a "metropolitan community."

The tendency to define metropolitan boundaries by function reinforces the functional concept of the metropolitan problem. In turn, efforts to stimulate awarness of a need for general governmental reorganization give way to concentration on techniques of functional problem solving. Metropolitan problems and metropolitan action become identified with specific government activities. State officials reflect the prevailing functional emphasis in their dealings with localities. Torn between local demands for general legislation only and conflicting demands that specific functional problems be solved individually, they have been hesitant to do more than suggest alternative patterns of local reorganization, while increasing state supervisory relations with local units through the state's own highly specialized and often uncoordinated maze of executive agencies.

THE UPSTATE METROPOLITAN AREAS

Notwithstanding the difficulties it presents, the Census Bureau definition can be used, with qualifications, to identify the outermost limits of those sections of the state where metropolitan problems have emerged to challenge existing local governmental capacities.

Buffalo—Niagara Falls. The position of Niagara Falls within this area is a subject of some confusion. The Temporary Commission on the Revision and Simplification of the Constitution commissioned a separate report on metropolitan Niagara County in 1957. Previous to 1960, the Census Bureau listed both Buffalo and Niagara Falls as central cities but subsequently changed the latter's position and the area's title to reflect more adequately the larger city's dominance. The pre-1960 joint listing is used here and in the accompanying tables, primarily to highlight the continued growth of Niagara Falls.

Buffalo and a strip development extending northward to the falls form almost one continuous urban settlement, serving as the hub of this metropolitan area. Local problems are complicated by extensive international, national, and state participation in water resource activities in the falls, river, and lakeshore areas.

Rochester. The state's third largest city is the center of a metropolitan area bounded by Monroe County. It shares with the Binghamton Area to the south the advantages or disadvantages of relative isolation from other major urban centers. The city and county enjoy a tradition of mutual confidence and cooperation, rarely interrupted by the major urban-suburban disputes characteristic of less politically stable communities.

Syracuse. The addition of Madison and Oswego Counties to the Syracuse Area reflects the impact of highways upon metropolitan growth. Syracuse lies at the junction of the New

York State Thruway and the Empire State Expressway. Although Onondaga County is far from completely urban, continued industrial dispersion portends even greater future development for it and its neighboring counties.

Albany-Schenectady-Troy. Saratoga County was added to this S.M.S.A. in 1960. Because of the timing of this research, Saratoga, as well as Madison and Oswego, will not be considered metropolitan counties in subsequent chapters. The capital area presents the most obvious picture of complex metropolitan development in upstate New York. The tricities and the counties in which they are contained, Albany, Schenectady, and Rensselaer, are highly interdependent. The counties share common resources. They are small in area and densely populated. Patterns of commutation are extensive and varied. The location of the state capital in Albany and the domination of the area by strong political organizations of differing party allegiance further complicate the area's political structure.

Binghamton. In some respects the Binghamton Area, composed of the city and Broome County, is the most difficult in which to obtain intergovernmental cooperation and agreement. Unlike other metropolitan areas in which population outside the city is just beginning to equal or surpass that of the central city, approximately 65 per cent of Broome County's population is located outside Binghamton. This population (of more than 130,000) is largely concentrated in the villages of Endicott and Johnson City and the town of Vestal. These jurisdictions retain forms of organization and attitudes toward governmental responsibility that make adaptation to the urban problems they and the city share very difficult.

Utica-Rome. The cities of Utica and Rome are both located in Oneida County. The proximity of a number of older municipalities and "dormitory" communities on its western edge have caused the inclusion of Herkimer County in the metropolitan area. Herkimer accounts for more than one-third of the population residing outside of the central cities.

With the exception of Binghamton, the metropolitan areas follow the "water-level" route across central New York, from Albany to Buffalo, formerly marked by the Erie Canal and now followed by the New York Central Railroad and the New York State Thruway. Many expect the Thruway to stimulate a ribbon of urban and industrial development all along its path. Because of topographical differences, the possibility of a similar north-south axis developing along the route of the Empire State Expressway, linking Watertown, Syracuse, and Binghamton, is considered more remote.

To date, the Thruway's impact has been most noticable in the merging of the Syracuse and Utica-Rome S.M.S.A.'s. The fortuitous location of five Thruway interchanges, plus an excellent strip of U.S. 20, between the two major cities accounts primarily for this phenomenon.

The upstate urban centers lend themselves to no ready political characterization. If anything, they tend to contradict the stereotype of central cities and surrounding counties dominated by different political parties. They have shown varied evidence of political agreement and disagreement, but none has yet to approach the improbable position of pitting a Republican city against a Democratic county.

STATE RECOGNITION OF THE METROPOLITAN PROBLEM

Concentration of population in and around the larger upstate cities has long occupied the state's attention. Numerous acts granting extraterritorial jurisdiction to city agencies, the creating of special multijurisdictional authorities, and the granting of urban powers to towns such as Union and Vestal illustrate early attempts to deal with problems arising from urban sprawl. But it was not until quite recently that any general concept of a metropolitan area and its problems was applied to upstate communities. Indeed, until the 1940's the term metropolitan, when used in New York State, usually referred only to the New York City area.

Recent state concern for the metropolitan problem was clearly expressed in the appointment of the Joint Legislative Committee on Metropolitan Areas Study in 1957. But New York enjoys a remarkable heritage of governmental research, dating almost from the turn of the century, that deals more or less directly with the same problems that are now of such great concern.

A history of New York State's governmental studies has yet to be written. It could well serve to illustrate the development of public administration theory in the United States. Many of the personalities identified with the public administration movement presented their thoughts in reports to New York State legislative committees and study commissions. The reports and action resulting from them can also be used to trace the impact of changing social and political philosophies upon American government.

In addition to the continuing programmatic research efforts of its executive agencies, New York State employs two major devices for fact finding, the legislative committee and the temporary commission. Both are usually temporary devices, although some have lasted for many years, and both enjoy great flexibility in organization and purpose. The temporary commission (the word temporary is often omitted from the title) usually draws its membership from local governmental and non-governmental sources and the executive branch of the state government, as well as the state legislature. The commission is usually employed where the subject under consideration requires an extensive public information campaign or where a greater appearance of objectivity or non-partisanship is required.[2]

There has been a noticeable difference in temper and manner of presentation between the legislative committee and temporary commission reports of the 1920's and 1930's and their more recent counterparts. With the exception of the staff reports prepared for the Temporary Commission on the Revision and Simplification of the Constitution, contemporary printed reports invariably present only the collective conclusions of the commission or committee. The earlier commission reports in particular usually included staff papers and departmental memoranda as well. Through these one could trace a proposal or line of reasoning from its inception in a paper by a staff member or noted consultant to its acceptance or rejection by the commission and its individual members.

The earlier works are sprinkled with bold and provocative proposals, argumentative reasoning and vigorous dissents. In contrast, contemporary reports seem to reflect a determination to avoid conflict and to present only those conclusions to which everyone can agree. Nevertheless, they continue to provide valuable insights into the development of past and present attitudes and policies in regard to government in general and metropolitan area problems in particular.

A number of historic studies and proposals have dealt with issues directly relevant to metropolitan problems in upstate New York. Three groups of studies can serve to exemplify trends in New York's approach to the emerging and now mature metropolitan problem. The first consists of the work of the Senate Committee on Taxation and Retrenchment and its successor, the Joint Special Committee on Taxation and

[2] Legislative methods of fact finding and policy development, with particular regard to the use of committee and commission, are described by Phillips Bradley, "Interlocking Collaboration in Albany," *Public Administration Review,* XVII, No. 3 (Summer, 1957), pp. 180–188.

Retrenchment. The second group of related studies includes the reports of the Commission for the Revision of the Tax Laws, the Commission on State Aid to Municipal Subdivisions, and the New York State Planning Council. Together these two groups of studies represent an almost continuous review of New York's governmental operations, with particular emphasis on taxation from 1916 to 1938. The third group of studies is that conducted by the Joint Legislative Committee on Metropolitan Areas Study, since its appointment in 1957.

Taxation and Retrenchment. It has been suggested that metropolitan problems were first experienced in New York State only after 1920, when the flow of population into central cities began to subside relative to growth in the suburbs.[3] Consequently, prior to the 1920's the most serious governmental problems were those associated with the central cities' adjustments to expanding population. State thinking at this time clearly distinguished urban from rural areas and needs. Urban areas (cities and some large villages) could well profit from new theories of organization and management, but for the most part rural areas could continue to discharge their limited responsibilities through the elective and administrative structures designed for them in the eighteenth century.

The concern for municipal problems at this time was the product of three forces: population growth and resulting demands upon city governments for increased services; state and local interest in reform and professionalism in government, motivated largely by nationwide exposures of corruption and mismanagement; and a related movement for economy in government in the face of anticipated increased service demands and alleged past extravagances.

Economy motived the appointment of the Committee on

[3] State of New York, Joint Legislative Committee on Metropolitan Areas Study, *1959 Report,* Legislative Document No. 19 (1959), p. 23.

Taxation and Retrenchment. State expenditures were its primary concern, but the committee found it necessary to relate the state's revenue and expenditure patterns to the general structure and operations of local government. In pursuit of its objectives, the committee examined the state and local tax system, local governmental organization and functions, the growth of state functions and expenditures, and the impact of the increasing use of state grants-in-aid and tax-sharing devices upon the state's financial condition.

A recurrent theme in the committee's deliberations was the fear that local taxation was placing an undue burden on property holders. In general, the committee endorsed the use of shared taxes and grants to alleviate the local property tax burden. But it sought to strengthen local governments so as to avoid excessive use of these devices and to check the growing tendency for the state government to engage in direct program expenditures.

Municipal home rule was viewed as one means of reducing state financial participation in local affairs. The Home Rule Amendment to the state constitution was enacted during the life of the Committee on Taxation and Retrenchment. For the first time, municipalities were empowered to enact their own charters and local laws, within the vague limits of state control that are still being tested judicially. Reorganization and professionalization of municipal service, through such innovations as the appointment of city managers, were regarded as major steps toward enabling cities to meet their expanding obligations. The committee also took some tentative steps toward recommending local reorganization and transfers of functions between town and county governments. But for the most part its recommendations were limited to problems of state and municipal finance and organization.

Until its dissolution in 1930, the Committee on Taxation

and Retrenchment was primarily concerned with studying means of reducing and redistributing tax burdens. In philosophy the committee did not favor curtailing governmental operations, preferring rather to make them more efficient. In fact, the committee often called for greater public expenditures, particularly for health, welfare, and highways. Wherever possible, it favored action through local initiative, rather than through the assumption of added duties by the state. But the growth of state expenditures continued and the minor revisions introduced during the 1920's failed to avert local government's growing reliance on the state for financial aid.

State Aid. In 1936, the Commission on State Aid to Municipal Subdivisions reported that the growth of state aid and the continuing pressures for more funds from Albany were traceable to local desires for increased services in the face of resistance to increases in property taxes. Grants and other payments were only one manifestation of the state's response to local pressure. In addition to increasing payments to localities, the state had steadily expanded the range of its own operations, partially to take the financial pressure off local units and partially as a result of evidence of local inability to provide needed services.[4]

Tax Revision. The Commission for the Revision of the Tax Laws was appointed in 1930 to continue the studies of the Committee on Taxation and Retrenchment. In addition to studying state and local governmental revenue and tax structures, the commission was authorized to review and comment upon state-local fiscal relations. The commission never accepted the view of one of its members that its objectives necessitated a complete study of governmental operations. Nevertheless, in its later years, it devoted an increasing

[4] State of New York, Commission on State Aid to Municipal Subdivisions, *Report,* Legislative Document No. 58 (1936), p. 5.

amount of attention to program operations, rather than limiting itself solely to financial problems. Even in one of its earlier reports, the commission felt compelled to comment that "both the town and the school district are too small for efficient and economical administration."[5] Although it would not go to the lengths some of its professional staff did in condemning town government, the commission did ask, "has the town outlived its usefulness as a unit of local government and should it be abolished and its functions transferred to the county?"[6]

In its 1932 report, the commission made what, if implemented, might have been its most far-reaching recommendation. It called for the creation of a local government board in Albany with substantial powers to review local budgeting and finance. The suggestion was patterned after the North Carolina model, in which broad discretionary authority was granted to a local government board.[7] While some of these duties have since been assigned to the Department of Audit and Control, the philosophy attending them has concentrated upon the technical and legal aspects of local finance rather than the policy aspects envisioned by the commission.

By 1935, the commission's perspective had broadened considerably, and it acknowledged the need to delve deeper into the non-financial aspects of state and local government. The attainment of an equitable tax structure was regarded as dependent upon a more fundamental objective, that of having "each unit of local government in New York State perform those functions in which it can perform most efficiently and most economically."[8]

---

[5] State of New York, Commission for the Revision of the Tax Laws, *Second Report, Part One: Summary of Conclusions and Recommendations,* Legislative Document No. 62 (1932), p. 238.

[6] *Ibid.,* p. 18.

[7] *Ibid.,* pp. 13–15.

[8] State of New York, Commission for the Revision of the Tax Laws,

To achieve a desirable redistribution of functions, the commission recommended among other means:

1. Transferring health and welfare to counties
2. Eliminating elected town highway superintendents and their appointment by county highway officials
3. The assumption of all police activities outside cities and villages by the state
4. Granting home rule to counties, both as a means of strengthening county government and as a device for facilitating additional transfers of function
5. Stimulating joint service arrangements and contracts between several units of government
6. Enforcing more restrictive debt limitations
7. Prohibiting the formation of additional special districts.[9]

Of the commission's major recommendations, only the transfer of welfare has come close to implementation. A number of counties have created county health departments, several have availed themselves of the limited home rule first granted them through constitutional amendment in 1935, and state policy has continually been liberalized to enable localities to engage in cooperative undertakings.

County government figured prominently in the commission's deliberations. The hint of reorganization and strengthening of county government suggested in the taxation and retrenchment studies blossomed into the Commission on Tax Revision's most repeated and unequivocal recommendation. The commission helped champion the optional county-charter system, outlined in the Home Rule Amendment of 1935. But the results of its efforts were disappointing. Counties have in fact been reluctant to take advantage of the several forms of government made

---

Sixth Report: Reorganization of Local Government, Legislative Document No. 63 (1935), p. 30.

[9] Summarized from *Ibid.*, pp. 16–25.

available to them by the legislature. Only two of the upstate metropolitan counties have done so,[10] but reorganization has not been accompanied by the wholesale transfers of functions to the county that had been contemplated by the supporters of the amendment and undoubtedly feared by its opponents. The significant increase in county activity during the past twenty years has generally occurred independently of the movement for county-government reorganization.

After the presentation of its tax program in 1932 and 1933, the commission continually broadened its scope of inquiry into the capabilities and problems of local governments. In 1937, the commission addressed itself specifically to the metropolitan problem in its study of *Financial Control in the Suburban Areas of New York State*.[11] Because of the commission's predominant interest in financial solvency, its major emphasis fell upon local tax structures. Focusing upon the financial difficulties of the state's larger urban centers and their suburbs, the commission repeated its call for the creation of a local government control board. But with Thomas H. Reed as its principal consultant, the commission went further than any previous or subsequent official body in tracing the problems of local governments in metropolitan areas to the multiplicity of local units and in recommending reduction in the number of units as the ultimate solution to their financial and functional problems.

One statement from the 1937 report warrants particular attention today. In a manner that has come to be part of the standard format of metropolitan studies, the commission reviewed the several methods developed for dealing with problems transcending jurisdictional boundaries. Although the

[10] Monroe and Erie Counties.

[11] State of New York, Commission for the Revision of the Tax Laws, *Tenth Report,* Legislative Document No. 63 (1937).

commission favored governmental integration and reorganization, it called for continuation of contractual and other forms of interlocal cooperation, regarding them possibly as "[serving] as a transition stage to more adequate units through [demonstration of] the advantages of cooperative efforts."[12]

Premature Subdivision. One of the principal motivations of the commission's metropolitan study was the evident impact of premature subdivision on local government solvency. The commission hoped to forestall repetition of the unfortunate circumstances in which most urban areas found themselves during the Depression through increased financial control from Albany and greater planning activity on the part of county governments. A more direct attack on the problem of land-use control in urban areas, however, came from a contemporary study of premature subdivision, conducted for the short-lived New York State Planning Council by Philip Cornick.[13]

New York's land boom of the 1920's, while not as spectacular as some, nevertheless involved large amounts of territory and money. Speculation in land subdivision had resulted in tax defaults on undeveloped and partially improved lots. In many instances, local governments had begun to extend facilities to lots in anticipation of home construction, only to be faced with tax delinquencies on the benefitted properties.

The effects of premature subdivision were evident throughout the state, but the greatest amount of speculation had occurred in and around the larger cities. For his study, Cornick selected a number of populous areas that coincided generally with those studied by the Commission for the Revision of the Tax Laws. He found tax delinquency very high in both the cities and their surrounding suburbs, but the towns had been

---

[12] *Ibid.*, p. 187.

[13] Philip H. Cornick, *Premature Subdivision and its Consequences* (New York: Institute of Public Administration, Columbia University, 1938).

particularly hard hit, since many of them had undertaken excessive commitments and had overextended their financial resources.

Cornick concluded that the town was unable to plan and control subdivision and that it was incapable of providing urban services to newly developed areas efficiently and economically. He found that the extraterritorial powers previously granted Syracuse and Rochester for the control of fringe-area land use had been neglected. The only effective alternative to extraterritorial power, as he saw it, was to absorb surrounding areas into the central municipalities (cities and villages) by annexation. To this end, Cornick recommended that towns be prohibited from borrowing for urban improvements.

Cornick pointedly ignored the county as a unit of service or as a device for achieving area coordination. He had no faith in extraterritorial devices, in cooperative means of assessing or approving development plans, or in state supervision of local activities. He reduced the problem to a basic formula: the fulfillment of urban needs requires an urban governmental organization. Although he suggested incorporation as one means of strengthening towns, Cornick favored annexations to cities rather than the formation of competing municipalities within metropolitan areas. Needless to say, the results of his study were generally ignored by the legislature.

Metropolitan Areas Study. The attitude of the Joint Legislative Committee on Metropolitan Areas Study can be said to revert back to that of the Retrenchment Committee. The committee's formula seems to be that of strengthening rather than replacing or reorganizing existing units of government. If not proven, that formula certainly has been tested in the past twenty years. Almost as if in deliberate disregard of earlier criticisms of towns, the legislature has continually broadened the range of activities in which they may engage, supplying them with more money and facilitating their entrance into interjurisdictional contracts and joint undertakings.

The Joint Legislative Committee on Metropolitan Areas Study was appointed in 1957 with Senator John Hughes, of Onondaga County, as its chairman. The committee believed that it was not altogether accurate to speak of "the metropolitan problem." It intended rather to study issues which were creating difficulties in metropolitan areas. The committee perceived those issues as falling into two broad classifications: the problems of the metropolitan core, and those of the still-developing suburban fringe. Although the problems were not deemed identical, they were traced to a common cause.

> Metropolitan problems are really the problems of growth or adjustment in populous urban centers, of matching financial resources with service requirements, and of adequate governmental organization. Certainly metropolitan problems are present wherever governmental services cannot be brought to representative standards of performance by reason of the fiscal, administrative, or jurisdictional limitations upon primary units of government acting individually within a metropolitan area.[14]

The committee's recommendations were intended to improve local governmental organization, foster and facilitate the use of interlocal service agreements and other devices for cooperation, and provide for increased state technical and financial assistance to local governments.

The committee's treatment of local government organization is particularly revealing of current legislative attitudes toward its role in metropolitan reorganization and toward local government in general. The committee cautioned:

> It should be borne in mind that in Article IX of the State Constitution, counties, cities, villages, and towns are recognized

[14] State of New York, Joint Legislative Committee on Metropolitan Areas Study, *1958 Report,* Legislative Document No. 30 (1958), p. 27.

or enumerated as the primary units of local government in New York State. However broad the powers of the Legislature, it is within this basic framework that the functions and responsibilities of local government must be distributed.

The Legislature is charged with the duty of providing for the organization of counties, cities, and villages and this mandate carries with it a limitation against creating other civil subdivisions vested with similar powers. There are constitutional restrictions upon the extent to which the primary units can be shorn of their existing powers by the creation of new agencies of local government.[15]

Without questioning the committee's interpretation of Article IX, it is worth noting that the committee and the legislature often claim credit for having championed and secured amendments to the constitution, where prohibitions affected less politically dangerous matters than the basic organization of local governments.

The committee believed that the county could become a more active service unit for the entire area within the existing structure and patterns of relationships of local governments. The committee found a number of examples of counties acting in this capacity and expected them to assume more functions at such time when community standards would accept nothing less than area-wide uniformity.[16] Should the state attempt to hasten or to influence local desires for area uniformity? Apparently not, in the committee's opinion. The state could facilitate uniformity by extending home-rule powers and revoking existing restrictive legislation, but it was not to interfere with the local responsibility for determining which functions require uniform treatment and when.

The committee favored extending home rule to urban towns;

---

[15] Joint Legislative Committee on Metropolitan Areas Study, *1959 Report, op. cit.*, p. 43.

[16]. *Ibid.*

for more responsible and better equipped towns could more adequately cope with those service demands that had not yet reached the stage where community standards required area-wide uniformity. But home rule cannot sweep away the financial and physical limitations under which local governments operate. As a corollary to strengthening local government, the committee favored the continued and expanded use of interjurisdictional agreements. To this end the committee (1) distributed a digest of state laws permitting interjurisdictional cooperation to local officials, many of whom were ignorant of the large and varied number of activities in which joint participation was possible, (2) distributed a pamphlet describing significant metropolitan action already in effect in six counties as examples of solutions locally enacted, (3) sponsored successfully a number of acts to permit joint participation and cost sharing in certain improvement projects and to eliminate legislative and constitutional restrictions on cooperative undertakings, and (4) introduced legislation serving as a blanket authorization for municipalities to enter into agreements for the joint performance of any activity which each of the participants is empowered to undertake alone.[17]

Strengthening the ability of local governments to act in their own behalf and permitting them to cooperate with one another in joint undertakings were the major legislative proposals stemming from the committee's hearings and deliberations. But the committee recognized that the state had metropolitan responsibilities beyond that of aiding local governments to help themselves. The committee recommended that an Office for

---

[17] A review of the committee's three years of activity is contained in State of New York, Joint Legislative Committee on Metropolitan Areas Study, *1960 Report* (mimeographed, March 21, 1960). The digest and pamphlet are, respectively, *Municipal Cooperation: A Digest of New York State Law* (1959), and *Metropolitan Action: A Six County Inventory (1960)*.

Local Government be established in the Governor's Executive Office. This agency was to serve as an advisor, expediter, and channel of communication between state and federal agencies and local governments. Since its duties were to be of an advisory nature, the committee recommended that the agency be headed by an appointed commission.

The Office for Local Government was added to the Executive Office, in different organizational form, as the result of a reorganization proposal submitted to the legislature by the Governor. However, the agency has retained the advisory purposes enunciated by the Committee. It is still too soon to attempt an evaluation of its effectiveness. The agency has experienced staffing difficulties. Local officials are uncertain of what it is to do for them, particularly in light of the complementary, if not similar activities, in which the Department of Audit and Control still engages. Some local officials have suggested, not all together facetiously, that they will be guided in their dealings with the two agencies by the fact that Audit and Control is the last Democratic stronghold in a Republican state government.

PRESENT METROPOLITAN POLICY

The sentiments of the Joint Legislative Committee on Metropolitan Area Problems are representative of current legislative understanding of the metropolitan problem. This committee regards that problem as the sum of a number of functional difficulties attending the provision of basic governmental services to large populations concentrated in and around the state's largest cities. Resolution of these difficulties may require some adjustment in the distribution of responsibilities among the primary units of local government. The timing and nature of these adjustments are deemed to be matters of local prerogative, subject to constitutional and legislative guidelines.

In the committee's view, the state's contribution to solutions of metropolitan problems should consist of aiding localities to increase their ability to deal with their own problems by removing restrictions on their ability to act and by making available to them the state's greater technical and, in some cases, financial resources. This concept of the state's role is certainly not one of vigorous, forceful leadership. Instead it depicts a state government waiting for localities to institute change. In fact, however, the legislative and executive branches of state government have done and are doing much more to promote and encourage metropolitan action. Their efforts follow no calculated or predetermined policy toward metropolitan areas but are a reaction to the daily operating problems of state and local officials in areas of metropolitan growth. From these actions, more than from legislative pronouncements, can be gleaned New York State's metropolitan policy.

III

Water Pollution Control

INADEQUATE WASTE DISPOSAL is a primary cause of water pollution. Adequacy of waste disposal depends upon the existence and effectiveness of a conveyance system (sewers) and the degree of treatment afforded waste. In the sense of cause and effect, water pollution does not stem from the existence of metropolitan areas. It is, however, affected by the degree of urbanization and the patterns of industrial allocation within a watershed area. In so far as the multiplicity of governments within densely populated areas complicates waste conveyance and disposal practices within watershed areas, water pollution becomes yet another metropolitan problem.

New York State has recently launched a major program of pollution abatement and control. To assume that this program has been undertaken as a result of current concern for metropolitan problems would overlook the more than fifty years of state activity in this field. It is more accurate to suggest that increasing metropolitan growth has added new emphasis and complexities to a problem long recognized in highly urban New York State.

---

[1] State of New York, Joint Legislative Committee on Interstate Cooperation, *1949 Report of the Special Committee on Pollution Abatement,* Legislative Document No. 51 (1949), p. 22.

Unlike many other problems attributed to metropolitan areas, the problem of water pollution and sewage disposal is often physically evident and obviously demanding a solution. No prescient survey is required to illustrate the interdependence of a village, swollen in population by central-city exodus, whose overburdened treatment plant discharges to a river; the city through which the river flows; and the downstream town whose public beach is becoming contaminated. Public awareness of pollution is relatively easily stimulated. However, although polluters are often readily identified, solutions are difficult to achieve. Unlike many other state activities, a program of pollution control, if effective, must alter existing local practices within metropolitan areas.

PAST METHODS OF POLLUTION CONTROL

New York State first took steps to control pollution at the turn of the twentieth century. Because water pollution affects both human beings and fish and wildlife, both the Health Department and the successive state agencies concerned with conservation were given concurrent regulatory responsibilities for preventing and abating pollution. The Department of Conservation and its predecessors concentrated their attention on industrial dischargers. Although the Health Department was not precluded from also dealing with industrial waste, it concerned itself primarily with sanitary sewage discharges. The two agencies cooperated in their complementary programs and shared the common hindrance of restrictive authorizing legislation narrowly construed by the courts.

In retrospect it is difficult to decide which department was more frustrated in its enforcement efforts. Although the Conservation Department enjoyed a relatively clear standard upon which to base its proceedings—dead fish are easily recognizable—it could act only after a harmful discharge. The difficulty of attributing a fish kill to any one discharge and the probability that the offending discharger would vary his practices, coupled with small penalties extracted if the case was won, hindered the department at every turn.

The Health Department was able to practice preventive, as well as punitive control. Dischargers of waste "in quantities injurious to public health" were required to obtain permits from the Commissioner of Health. He was empowered to institute court action when discharges threatened health or constituted a public menace. The court's insistence that for purposes of the Public Health Law, pollution be defined as a condition "injurious to public health," however, proved to be the department's major difficulty. Since industrial waste discharges are rarely directly injurious to human health, the department was forced to concentrate on sanitary sewage discharges, and then only in instances of gross pollution.[2]

In 1932, the Health Department was also empowered to review and approve subdivision plans for the adequacy of their waste-disposal systems. First applicable to subdivisions of two or more plots, later to five or more, subdivision control has come to be one of the state's major tools of pollution prevention and indeed of metropolitan planning. Unfortunately, the state's capacity to exercise effective controls over subdivisions and waste discharges has often been rendered ineffective by rigid judicial interpretation, lack of cooperation by local authorities, and, at times, local officials' conspiring with violators.

The inadequacies of existing controls stimulated demands for a new approach to pollution abatement as early as 1924.[3]

---

[2] The difficulties encountered by the two departments are reviewed in State of New York, Joint Legislative Committee on Interstate Cooperation, *Progress Report of the Special Committee on Pollution Abatement,* Legislative Document No. 59 (1947), pp. 30–43.

[3] State of New York, Conservation Commission, *Thirteenth Annual Report,* Legislative Document No. 30 (1924), pp. 236–239, calls for creation of a quasilegislative body with antipollution powers similar to those given to the Water Pollution Control Board in 1949.

The Water Pollution Control Act of 1949 created a new pollution-control agency, the Water Pollution Control Board, but reaffirmed the previous authority of the Health and Conservation Departments pending review of the program in 1959, a target date subsequently extended.

LEGISLATIVE ACTION

On March 26, 1946, alarmed at increasing evidence of pollution throughout the state and influenced by pending federal water-pollution legislation, the State Legislature directed its Joint Legislative Committee on Interstate Cooperation to appoint a Special Committee on Pollution Abatement. The Special Committee was reappointed annually until 1951, when its duties were assigned to the newly formed Joint Committee on Natural Resources. To one unfamiliar with the committee system in New York, the activities of the two committees would seem to negate the state constitutional requirement of separation of powers. Reviewing the program of the Special Committee, the Natural Resources Committee counted among its achievements:

> Enactment of the Water Pollution Control Law.
>
> Development of increased interest in water pollution control on the part of industrial and municipal officials and of groups of individuals, to a greater extent than [had] ever been experienced in New York State.
>
> Focusing of attention on the need for research in industrial wastes treatment and utilization and for equitable fiscal responsibilities of industries and municipalities.[4]

Among its continuing objectives, the Natural Resources Committee sought to

> cooperate with the Water Pollution Control Board by appropriate legislative liaison activities and by active support of its technical,

---

[4] State of New York, Joint Legislative Committee on Natural Resources, *1956 Report*, Legislative Document No. 63 (1956), p. 222.

survey, classification and standardization program; by study of its laws and procedures; and by aiding in its relations with the public, municipalities and industry.[5]

The committee also intended to "press for," "encourage," and "stimulate" cooperative approaches to disposal problems through integrated planning, financing, and construction of waste works.

The committee's words should not be construed as mere legislative verbiage. Any review of the operation of the pollution-control program during the past ten years cannot relegate the committees to a chapter on background and legislative history. In a number of ways, the Natural Resources Committee and, during its existence, the Special Committee have contributed as much to the program as the Water Pollution Control Board. Their participation can be summarized under three headings:

1. *Public Relations.* The initial publicity surrounding the hearings and deliberations of the Special Committee and the continued support given to the Water Pollution Control Board by the legislative committees have served to keep the issue of pollution abatement before the public and have paved the way for the board's regulatory activities.

2. *Legislative Direction.*

a. The committees have maintained active liaison with the Water Pollution Control Board, guiding necessary legislative changes in its program.

b. The committees have also helped to steer a number of measures indirectly relating to the pollution program and to the fiscal capacity of municipalities to pursue their objectives through the legislature. Several of these measures offer significant opportunities for changes in metropolitan organization.

3. *Program Participation.* In at least two situations, the

[5] *Ibid.,* p. 223.

Long Island Duck Waste dispute and the Buffalo River Project, the two committees worked along with the Board. They participated in conferences, research, and direct negotiations with the interested parties.

The Special Committee's first task was to inventory sewage works needed in the state. Its findings indicated a general lack of adequate facilities and a need for new facilities in several hundred municipalities. New construction alone was estimated to require an expenditure of more than 400 million dollars.[6] The enormity of the financial problem was of special concern to municipal leaders and to the Conference of Mayors. Throughout its well attended hearings and in all its subsequent deliberations, the Special Committee was constantly reminded that its work could lead to the mandating of sewage works construction which local governments might not be able to finance.

Accordingly, the committee's first recommendations were for further study of local financial potential and for the continuation of a wartime planning grant that had been slated to end. The planning-grant program was reinstituted in 1947 under the sponsorship of the Special Committee. It provided, on a matching basis, for a state contribution of up to 2 per cent of construction costs for the preparation of preliminary and detailed plans for sewage construction. Similar legislation offered loans of up to 4 per cent of construction costs to sewer authorities.

The impact of the grant program is hard to measure. True, fifty-three applications for grants were received in less than three years after its reactivation. They offer some justification for the Committee's contention that the program stimulated interest in sewage construction. But some planning probably

---

[6] Joint Legislative Committee on Interstate Cooperation, *Progress Report of the Special Committee on Pollution Abatement, op. cit.*, p. 141.

would have been undertaken without the offer of state funds and the credit claimed by the Water Pollution Control Board for stimulating increased construction through its enforcement program also seems to detract from the effect attributed to the grant program. It is likely, however, that the financial stimulus did influence several marginal municipalities. Fourteen of the first fifty-three applications received were from municipalities reported by the Comptroller to be unable to finance construction, because of constitutional tax or debt limitations.

By far the Special Committee's most significant achievement was its sponsorship of the Water Pollution Control Act. But the committee and its successor have also been instrumental in the passage of a number of constitutional and statutory changes that promise to have a lasting effect on waste-disposal practices in metropolitan areas. These measures, inspired by financial considerations, were developed in cooperation with the Comptroller's Committee on Constitutional Tax and Debt Limitations and City-School Fiscal Relations.

Municipalities in New York State had long had the authority to contract for joint construction and operation of sewage collection and treatment systems. A related constitutional prohibition, however, mitigated the effectiveness of this tool of interlocal cooperation. Sections one and two of Article Eight of the State Constitution prohibited a municipality from giving or loaning its money to a public or private corporation and further prohibited it from incurring debt for other than municipal purposes. The intent to aid another municipality was not considered a municipal purpose by the courts. The effect of this interpretation was to require cash contributions and the sharing of debt by all parties contract to an agreement. Since the very municipalities that could benefit most through contractual arrangements with larger units usually were close to, if not at, their debt limits, joint projects could not be undertaken. Following a pattern previously used for developing water-supply systems, the committee sponsored and obtained a constitutional amendment enabling the legislature to authorize municipalities to incur debt to provide facilities in excess of their own needs for the purpose of contracting with other municipalities.[7] Speaking for the Comptroller's Committee on behalf of the amendment, Senators Horton and Milmoe said:

> We believe that this amendment and the implementing legislation will go far toward enabling counties, cities, towns and villages in New York State to meet one of the major remaining problems of metropolitan areas—the financing of sewage treatment facilities and drainage.[8]

For a time, the legislature had considered extending to sewage works the privilege previously afforded water supply of exclusion from debt limitation. This proposal was withdrawn, it appears, largely due to objection of the Comptroller's Committee. Although the Natural Resources Committee later questioned its logic, the Comptroller's Committee believed that a previous amendment authorizing advance partial exclusion from debt-limit computations of projects made self-sustaining through sewer-service or rental charges would enable municipalities to operate within their constitutional debt limitations.[9] The advance exclusion from debt limitation was, however, only partial and was dependent upon imposition of sewer charges or a rental system. Sewer-rental systems, although appealing in principle, have been very difficult to institute, particularly in contractual operations.

In 1954, the legislature amended the County Law in a

---

[7] State of New York, *Constitution,* Art. 8, sec. 2-a.

[8] Quoted in State of New York, Joint Legislative Committee on Natural Resources, *1955 Report,* Legislative Document No. 76 (1955), p. 144. Note the optimistic use of the phrase "remaining problems of metropolitan areas."

[9] State of New York, Joint Legislative Committee on Natural Resources, *1950 Report,* Legislative Document No. 74 (1950), p. 171.

manner which may have the most far reaching effect on metropolitan organization for sewage disposal. Counties were authorized to establish county sewer agencies or to appoint sewer officers. Under the direction of the Board of Supervisors, the agency or officer could create county sewer districts for the conveyance and disposal of sewage from sewage districts and municipalities within the county. Furthermore, county sewer districts could consist of non-contiguous territories, as long as the sewage system was to be interrelated or interdependent.[10]

This was the first general authorization for counties to enter into sewage programs. Through special legislation, similar powers had already been given to the urban counties of Westchester, Nassau, and Onondaga.

The 1954 general act was designed with the previous special legislation in mind, although it differed considerably from the earlier acts. It was specifically introduced as a result of a request from Broome County for similar authority.[11]

THE WATER POLLUTION CONTROL LAW OF 1949

Several features distinguish the Water Pollution Control Law from previous attempts at pollution control. Chief among these has been removal of the responsibility for defining pollution from the courts and its assignment to an administrative board. No longer is pollution subject to legal tests of nuisance or conditions "injurious to public health." Pollution is now defined as any discharge which lessens the quality of water below standards previously prescribed for a particular body of water by the Water Pollution Control Board. Thus, through its classifications, the board can effectively dictate the quality of treatment required of dischargers,[12] and through its permit-

---

[10] State of New York, *Laws of 1954,* C. 794, sec. 210.

[11] Memorandum of Senator Anderson in *McKinney's Session Laws of New York: 1954,* p. 1105.

[12] A. F. Dappert, Executive Secretary of the Board, would undoubtedly object to the statement in this form. It resembles the position of the City

issuance procedures and legal-enforcement powers, require dischargers to maintain water up to its standards.

The law seeks to prevent new pollution and to abate existing pollution through the maintenance of reasonable standards of purity for the state's waters. The board consists of the Commissioners of Health, Conservation, Agriculture and Markets, and Public Works. It has primary responsibility for pollution abatement and prevention. It is required to classify the state's waters, considering the best usage of water in the public interest and with regard to the following factors: (1) hydrologic factors; (2) character of district bordering the waters; (3) past, present, and foreseeable future uses of water, including transportation, water supply, recreational, industrial, etc.; (4) extent of present defilement.[13] The law recognizes that there is no single use or standard applicable to all waters. Within broad legislative intent, the board is free to adopt any classification for a particular body of water, subject to procedural provisions requiring hearings prior to final classification determinations.

By law, the board is required to follow six steps in its program:

1. Classification survey. This is done by drainage-basin area and includes all subbasins and tributaries to a major drainage outlet.

2. Published report of survey. The report contains tentative classifications recommended by the board's staff.

3. Classification hearings. The tentative classifications are

---

of Troy and the Village and Town of Waterford in their unsuccessful challenge of the Act's constitutionality. Dappert insists that the classification of water has nothing to do with dictating treatment. It merely reflects the public interest in regard to the best use of water. His argument is contained in a review of the Troy and Waterford cases in Joint Legislative Committee on Natural Resources, *1955 Report, op. cit.*, pp. 153–165.

[13] *McKinney's Consolidated Laws of New York Annotated*, vol. 44, par. 1208.

discussed at public hearings held at convenient locations within the drainage area.

4. Adoption of classifications by the board. The board may modify tentative classifications as a result of the hearing, but once the waters have been classified, "sewage or waste discharges which violate the standards specified for the class assigned the waters constitute pollution."[14]

5. Development of comprehensive pollution-abatement plans. The plan consists of a description of each pollutional problem within the area and the procedure to be followed in each instance to comply with the classification. Reports of progress in achieving compliance are required, and a reasonable time for correction is agreed upon.

6. Enforcement of the comprehensive plan. The board considers this step as consisting of two phases:

a. a cooperative phase and, if voluntary cooperation is not satisfactory,

b. the issuance of formal enforcement orders. Finally, if necessary, the Attorney General is notified to commence court proceedings.

The law also requires dischargers to apply to the board for permits to discharge. Since the Public Health Law still requires permits from the Commissioner of Health, permits are jointly issued at present. In 1953, the Water Pollution Control Law was amended to relieve operators of systems discharging less than 20,000 gallons per day or serving less than 200 people of the necessity of acquiring permits from the board, where local health officials can exercise adequate control or when effluents are satisfactorily discharged to ground waters.

---

[14] State of New York, Water Pollution Control Board, *Eight Years of Water Pollution Control Progress in New York State,* by A. F. Dappert (Albany: 1957), p. 15. The booklet contains a summary of the program from which these six steps have been taken.

The exceptions relating to ground waters and the decentralization of some control to local health officials were requested by the board. Although not specified in the original act, some decentralization had been considered by the Special Committee as early as 1949. In dealing with the problem of local pollution in unincorporated areas and the problem of ground-water contamination of surface waters, the Special Committee had drawn up a model local sanitation code in the belief that "the correction of such pollution conditions is a local problem which can best be handled by local officials in keeping with local practices and policies."[15]

Nevertheless, the present law makes no distinction between surface and ground waters, and it is expected that the board will proceed to classify ground waters in the not too distant future. At that time it will probably be necessary to review current legislative and administrative policies regarding septic tank regulation and subdivision control. These Health Department functions, currently coordinated with the board's activities through administrative rules, are a particularly important tool of pollution prevention in growing metropolitan areas.

A review of legislation enacted since the emergence of the state's new policy of pollution abatement indicates a continuing legislative recognition of the impact of a vigorous antipollution program upon metropolitan areas. To some extent, recent legislation has been designed specifically to soften that impact by enabling municipalities to select new forms of organization and finance for sewage disposal. Liberally sprinkled throughout the reports of the committees are references to the multi-governmental aspects of the pollution problem. Indeed, the Water Pollution Control Law itself requires the board to

encourage the formulation and execution of plans by cooperative

[15] Joint Legislative Committee on Interstate Cooperation, *1949 Report of the Special Committee on Pollution Abatement, op. cit.*, p. 63.

groups or associations of municipalities, industries and other users of the waters, who severally or jointly, are or may be the source of pollution in the same waters, for the prevention and abatement of pollution.[16]

But the law itself does not require or offer any inducement for metropolitan consideration of sewage disposal. It is in its administration that the law may serve to influence local governments toward joint action. As an expression of policy and a promise of enforcement, the law has stimulated further legislation offering local governments the opportunity to jointly approach their common sewage-disposal problems. Whether local governments accept the offer will depend upon their own awareness of their metropolitan status and the ability of the Water Pollution Control Board to impress that awareness upon them.

At the same legislative session in which the County Law was amended to provide for county sewer agencies, sections 1131-1141 of the Public Health Law were repealed. At the time of their passage in 1932, they were probably looked upon as a means of broadening jurisdictional capacities for sewage-disposal operations. They, too, authorized the formation of sanitary districts comprising several municipalities; but a complicated procedure of petitioning the court and submitting a proposition to the electorate had to be followed. Until the Health Department recommended their repeal in 1954, only one attempt had been made to use these provisions—and that one was eventually abandoned.[17] Fortunately, more recent enabling legislation utilizes less complicated procedures for local adoption, but the question of whether it will be used still remains.

---

[16] *McKinney's Consolidated Laws of New York Annotated,* Vol. 44, sec. 1208, par. 46.

[17] Memorandum of the State Department of Health in *McKinney's Session Laws of New York: 1954,* p. 1455.

Through its classification, consultative, and enforcement procedures the Water Pollution Control Board enjoys numerous opportunities for influencing and actually determining the nature of waste disposal activities within metropolitan areas. Its actions may lead to reorganization of local functions and redistributions of authority with varying degrees of permanence and importance. But, in general, the board is concerned neither with over-all problems of metropolitan areas nor with schemes for metropolitan government. It is concerned only with pollution abatement. Metropolitan cooperation is incidental to the board's objectives and enters into its consideration only within the context of pollution extending beyond the boundaries of individual governmental units.

The board's staff is primarily oriented toward the engineering aspects of public health. From an engineering perspective, a drainage basin is the logical geographical area of pollution control. Indeed, drainage basins are most often larger than the boundaries of metropolitan areas as defined demographically or for most functional purposes. However, the board welcomes metropolitan action, because it lessens the gap between the size of drainage areas and the jurisdictional limits of local governments and because it facilitates negotiation and enforcement of comprehensive plans. Wherever possible, the board stimulates and encourages joint or cooperative municipal activity; but it will not jeopardize the opportunity of stimulating technically acceptable action by independent units of government by insisting upon controversial political solutions. As illustrated by the following cases, its staff is guided by the adage about a bird in hand.

The Syracuse Case. In 1953, the board was preparing to classify Onondaga Lake and its tributaries. Prior to the classification hearings, the Executive Secretary met frequently with public officials and private citizens to advise them of what might be required by the board. Earlier work by the Departments of Health and Conservation and local study groups had relieved Mr. Dappert of the need to demonstrate the multigovernmental nature of the problem. In fact, there was already a great deal of local support in favor of some form of metropolitan action. To this sentiment Dappert added his voice and authority.

A number of plans for sewage treatment had been presented to local authorities by consulting engineers. The plans represented two basic alternatives: an interdependent treatment system linking the city and two county sewer districts, to be built and operated by the county Public Works Commission, or construction of two new separate plants to serve the city and county areas. The separate plants would probably have been built and operated independently of one another. The consulting engineers favored the metropolitan plan; but it contained several controversial features, including diversion of sewage effluent from the lake to the Seneca River.

Although the lake had not yet been classified, the consulting engineer requested Dappert's approval of the metropolitan plan and his help in promoting it. Dappert obliged by indicating approval, subject to certain modifications, and by assuring downstream Seneca River residents that the plan would not adversely affect them. In the months that followed, Dappert continued his support through appearances before local legislative bodies and citizen groups. His letter of acceptance, however, reveals the primary emphasis the board places on technical rather than political criteria in striving for pollution abatement. After indicating his personal preference for the metropolitan plan and expressing the belief that with modifications it would be approved by the board, he added, without having been asked, that the other plans under consideration would also be acceptable, although they did not call for metropolitan cooperation.

The Utica Case. Opinion differs in Onondaga County as to the importance of Dappert's support to the final acceptance of the metropolitan plan. The board itself refers to the role of its staff as merely having assisted local arrangements.[18] In the Utica area, the board reported a more active role:

> Encouragement has been given to the city of Utica and adjoining villages and towns to join together in solving of the sewage disposal problem of the Utica metropolitan area.[19]

The encouragement given in Utica came at a time when the Waterford and Troy cases were before the court. Municipalities in the Utica area were reluctant to take any action necessitating large expenditures, pending the outcome of the test cases. When the board's discretionary authority was confirmed by the court, its staff proceeded to prod local officials into developing a comprehensive and, hopefully, metropolitan plan. Unlike those in Onondaga County, the municipalities in the Utica area are politically divided and, to the disappointment of state officials, cooperative arrangements could not be worked out. The resulting comprehensive plan called for independent corrective action by a number of municipalities and industries. Although the plan is technically adequate for the present, the staff of the board and the Health Department still believe that greater economy and potential protection would have been realized through metropolitan action.

The Comprehensive Plan. The comprehensive plan is the foundation upon which the enforcement phase of pollution abatement and control rests. It cites each source of pollution within a drainage area and outlines the corrective action to be

[18] Joint Legislative Committee on Natural Resources, *1955 Report*, *op. cit.*, p. 152.

[19] *Ibid.*, p. 153.

taken by each polluter or potential polluter. It need not relate individual sources of pollution to each other or plan for collective objectives and actions. To the would-be integrator of metropolitan areas, this concept of comprehensiveness leaves something to be desired.

The plan reflects not only the demands of the board but also the willingness of polluters to take action. It is developed by the staff in consultation with local interests and is the result of negotiation and prior agreement. Thus, despite its own preference, the staff developed a non-metropolitan comprehensive plan for the Utica area, when it became obvious that cooperative action could no longer be expected. Similarly, the comprehensive plan for Onondaga Lake was not prepared until 1956, when all local parties had accepted the decision to take joint action.

Local Interests and the Board. The Water Pollution Control Board has had more success in conducting multilateral negotiations than did the Conservation or Health Departments. A deliberate policy of encouraging joint participation has been practiced by the board and by the Legislative Committees in their dealings with problem areas. The policy is implemented by the very manner in which the board prepares survey reports, conducts classification hearings, and emphasizes local participation in the development of comprehensive plans.

The survey reports have served to highlight multigovernmental contributions to pollution. In Onondaga County this emphasis, supplied previously by the Health and Conservation Departments, was instrumental in convincing suburban dwellers that they shared part of the responsibility for the pollution of Onondaga Lake. It was effective in bringing together municipal and industrial officials to discuss their common problems. The mere existence of the board served as a focal point for the convergence of numerous public and private interests which might otherwise not have been heard. Statutory authority enabled the board to exploit its central position by influencing the attitudes and plans of these often conflicting interests.

Despite Mr. Dappert's protestations, the classification of waters is probably the most important state activity contributing to determination of local sewage-disposal policies within a metropolitan area. The classification can effectively predetermine future private and governmental sewage disposal expenditures. The classification process presents a challenge to local discretion not present in earlier pollution control programs. To meet this challenge, local interests have attended classification hearings in force and in relative unity. The hearings have encouraged the particpation of governmental, business, manufacturer, and taxpayer groups. To the extent that mutual interest can be sustained and turned toward cooperative or joint planning and operations, the board can capitalize on the reaction to its challenge.

In its earlier manifestations, however, cooperation, or at least shared interest, is usually aimed at reducing potential costs by attaining the lowest possible classifications. Paradoxically, the political cooperation inspired by reaction to the classification process presents a threat to the board's technical objectives. The price of sustaining cooperative attitudes and relationships tends to be local acceptance of the cheapest, "most reasonable" course of action. The interaction of state classification, local interests, and cooperative attitudes toward sewage disposal is well illustrated by one of the arguments advanced by an advocate of the metropolitan sewage plan in Onondaga County. In a letter to county political leaders urging the county to undertake a metropolitan sewage-treatment program, its consulting engineer reported:

I believe I can say with assurance that local interests can deal with the Water Pollution Control Board with more satisfaction if one body can speak for all local interests. I have discussed the matter with representatives of the Water Pollution Control Board and I have been advised that the Board would accept a much more reasonable program of construction from one agency such as the [county] commission than is likely to be acceptable if the Water Pollution Control Board has to deal with two local agencies both of whom are involved in discharging pollution in one body of water such as Onondaga Lake.

Experience in Utica and Troy indicate that the "reasonableness" of a program acceptable from one rather than a number of agencies would not extend to the board's sacrificing its own interests and standards.

WATER-POLLUTION CONTROL IN THE FUTURE

After ten years, the results of the water-pollution control program indicate its relative success. Most of the state's surface waters have been classified. Comprehensive plans have been developed and are being enforced in places of most serious pollution. A review of procedures and the board's relations with the Departments of Health and Conservation is now under way. It should lead to reconsideration of the two aspects of a water-quality control program as yet ignored by the board: the regulation of ground-water discharges, and small surface-water discharges.

Both types of regulation are now exercised by the State Health Department, the former as a traditional aspect of subdivision and environmental control, the latter as a result of amendments to the Water Pollution Control Act sponsored by the board. They are of particular importance to the future development of metropolitan areas because of their impact upon the placement and construction of sewage-conveyance systems, as contrasted with the board's present emphasis on systems of treatment and disposal. Furthermore, the cumulative effect of small discharges and ground-water pollution may, if inadequately regulated, lead to pollution of the very surface waters upon which the board is now concentrating.

Through its regional and district offices, the State Health Department enforces a flexible program of subdivision, septic tank, and surface discharge regulation. The program rests upon the department's authority to review subdivision plans for adequacy of water and sewage facilities and to issue permits for discharges into surface waters. Because of variations in local soil and water conditions, the recommendations of field sanitary engineers are generally accepted as the basis for departmental action. Varying conditions are also reflected in the absence of departmental standards and the delegation of a great deal of discretion to field officials.

When the subdivision program was first begun in 1932, it was regarded as a significant tool for the orderly planning and development of suburban areas. It has been so used in a number of communities. In Onondaga County, a District Health Office policy requiring minimum lot sizes for the installation of septic tanks or the laying of dry sewers for future connection has helped to stimulate a ring of suburban disposal plants and sewage districts formed by developers or towns and developers cooperatively. Advance planning, extension of existing systems, and construction of facilities prior to building have resulted from the district policy and promise to ease the future impact of metropolitan growth.

The cooperation of town planning and zoning boards and developers was deemed vital to the program in 1932. It still is necessary to assure the submittal of all plans to health officials. Where cooperation has been attained, the subdivision control program has been an effective and important force in metropolitan development. Where towns and developers have sought to circumvent state requirements, the effectiveness of the program has been limited. Whether or not the review of present organization and procedures for pollution control will lead to more adequate methods of operation, it should result in a more concentrated attack on both the ground- and surface-water aspects of pollution.

CONCLUSION

The state's most fundamental contribution to eliminating pollution has been the publicity it has given the problem. This publicity serves an immediate metropolitan purpose by alerting local communities to their needs and responsibilities. In many instances, it has only been through incessant prodding by the Water Pollution Control Board or the Departments of Health or Conservation that local governments have even admitted their share in polluting a body of water.

No community likes to be identified as the polluter of a stream, river, or lake. When so accused, its leaders will almost inevitably point out other communities as the real culprits. Amid recriminations, suspicions, and distrust, each community hesitates to inaugurate an expensive sewage treatment or conveyance plan without assurances of similar action from its neighbors. State efforts at pollution abatement have pinpointed local responsibilities, provided a forum at which representatives of several communities could discuss their mutual problems, and served to assure area leaders and residents that action would be required of all of them.

The Water Pollution Control Board's success rests ultimately on the state's coercive power. Although the board considers coercion in the form of legal action to be a last resort, the possibility of its use is always present. Water-pollution control is a regulatory program. It offers some tactical and strategical advantages in dealing with local governments not present in the performance of service functions.

Control of subdivisions for adequacy of water supply, sewage conveyance, treatment, and disposal is also a regulatory function separate from, although complementary to, the water-pollution control program. Current development of the subdivision control program, however, seems in danger of losing one of the major advantages of state regulatory action as a device for metropolitan integration. The state is delegating responsibility for subdivision control to county health departments, where they exist.

It has already been suggested that the state can do much to bring local parties together merely by appearing on the scene as a relatively objective third party. Distance provides state officials not only with an appearance of impartiality but also with insulation from the excesses of local demands and interests. Distance also makes it easier to resort to coercion. By delegating subdivision control to county health departments, the state is deliberately reducing the distance between the regulating agency and local interests. This policy is motivated by reasons discussed in Chapter IV. Lack of sufficient experience permits only guesses as to whether subdivision control is more effective when locally enforced than when regulated from a distance.

At yet the state has not had to use coercion to enforce its program. Persuasion and encouragement are usually the tools with which state officials follow up their demands for action to abate or prevent pollution. Persuasion and encouragement are given to cooperative and joint action, but any local sewage disposal and treatment program will be approved if it serves to reduce pollution. The Water Pollution Control Board will insist upon metropolitan action only when adequate treatment cannot be assured through any other type of action. Usually, however, ten town treatment plants are as good as (if not better than) one metropolitan plant for keeping a stream clean.

Each of the ten towns, however, cannot afford the investment required in building sewage facilities. The anticipation of economy, although not always decisive, does much to support the state's preference for cooperative local action. But here too the state appears to be moving in directions that will minimize the current economic stimulants to metropolitan action.

In 1936, the Temporary Commission on State Aid to Municipal Subdivisions regarded conditional grants-in-aid as ineffective means of inducing particular local responses. Its report suggested, however, that if local communities could not be bought out, perhaps they could be starved out.[20] Many localities are now virtually being starved into submitting to joint or cooperative sewage programs. They cannot afford to "go it alone." In response to local complaints that the state is forcing them to spend more money without helping them to raise it, the Joint Legislative Committee on Metropolitan Areas Study supported a bill that would provide grants-in-aid for construction of sewage treatment and conveyance systems. Although the grant could be made conditional upon the submittal of cooperative or joint plants, this eventuality is highly unlikely considering the plan's motivation. The grant is not being considered as a stimulative device but rather as a means of providing tax relief for local governments. Indeed, as currently proposed, the grant would provide greater benefits to two communities acting independently than to a joint project, since a limit of $60,000 for any one project is being considered. The grant is thus potentially anti-integrative and promises to encourage small projects by smaller units of government.

A similar counterintegrative trend is evident in another legislative proposal to enable towns and villages to construct joint treatment facilities. In itself this proposal appears to open the way for greater cooperation, but in the long run it may

---

[20] Commission on State Aid to Municipal Subdivisions, *op. cit.,* p. 29.

forestall the eventual integration of area-wide sewage programs. The legislature and the Water Pollution Control Board both look to the county as the eventual agency of metropolitan sewage-program coordination. Steps have been taken to permit the county to occupy this role. But at the same time, the state is encouraging the formation of joint town-village districts, which may compete with county sewer agencies and prevent them from developing uniform waste disposal policies. In the same report in which it recommended village-town cooperation, the Joint Legislative Committee on Metropolitan Areas Study quoted approvingly a statement by a representative of the Onondaga Public Works Commission urging greater authority for county sewer agencies to develop master plans for sewage disposal and treatment.[21] The two seemingly counter trends in state policy appear to reflect differences in short-range and long-range approaches to sewage disposal and the metropolitan problem. Short-range objectives seek the immediate construction of additional facilities, preferably, but not necessarily, with a view toward cooperative action. The attainment of short-range objectives may make it more difficult to achieve the long-range goal of area-wide planning and direction.

As long as the state continues to view sewage treatment as a problem in itself rather than as a manifestation of the metropolitan problem, and as long as state responsibility is vested in an agency whose goals are immediate and operative and to whom long-range metropolitan considerations are secondary, state policy will probably continue to favor short-range objectives.

---

[21] Joint Legislative Committee on Metropolitan Areas Study, *1958 Report, op. cit.*, pp. 38–39.

IV

Public Health

FOR AS LONG as governments have been concerned with the health of their citizens, public-health officials have insisted that germs and diseases respect no political boundaries. In the nineteenth century, this slogan led to efforts to extend public-health services to all people, through programs conducted by numerous independent units of government. In our time, the same concept provides a foundation for metropolitan health programs.

Early state and national public-health programs had first to conquer a rural American prejudice that viewed cities alone as breeders of disease. Villages, towns, and unorganized areas too could benefit from protective community-health measures. Through the creation of thousands of local boards of health, minimal protection was eventually achieved. Inspired by early concepts of public health as an activity concerned with the prevention and isolation of communicable diseases, a pattern of decentralization particularly suited to the theory and reality of nineteenth century political organization was established. In turn, this pattern has helped perpetuate a philosophy of local self-sufficiency that has become increasingly less tenable.

Modern medical accomplishments have led to demands for public-health services that many, if not most, small administrative units are technically and financially unable to provide. Health statistics show a direct correlation between the size of the unit of administration and the results obtainable from preventive health techniques. Larger units can afford more diversified and professionalized programs and personnel. Almost forty years ago, public-health authorities recognized the inadequacy of small administrative units. The State of New York has ever since been promoting the absorption of many local health agencies into larger units.

Metropolitan growth has influenced the development of state policy in regard to local health units. Early public-health work centered in areas of population concentration. When attention was turned to rural needs, the county was considered an administrative unit particularly capable of providing public-health services to the residents of thinly settled, unincorporated places. In 1932, a special health commission noted that the service requirements of metropolitan areas presented problems very similar to those encountered in rural areas.[1] A county health agency seemed to offer a common solution.

Continued suburbanization results in population dispersions as well as concentrations. Densely settled suburban areas require health services fully comparable to those offered in central cities. The minimal programs conducted by older local units must be augmented to accommodate the influx of new residents, many of whom, recently moved from the city, expect a high level of public-health services. Newly developed fringe areas are presented with new needs and responsibilities. In a metropolitan area, a county health agency can provide new services to some communities and coordinate them with programs already developed in more urban sections. Since 1932,

---

[1] State of New York, Governor's Special Health Commission, *Public Health in New York State* (Albany: 1932), pp. 59–60.

the state has pressed for the creation of county health departments in both urban and rural areas.

In promoting the goal of fifty-seven county health departments, state policy has had to overcome disinterest, inertia, opposition, and the loyalty to a system previously created by the state itself. Resistance has most often been able to withstand change.

Public-health activities in New York State can be traced as far back as the eighteenth century. However, it was not until 1850 that a state-wide public-health program was organized. In that year, the state legislature required each city and incorporated village to appoint a board of health and a health officer. The appointment of health boards and health officers was optional for towns. In 1880, a State Board of Health with limited administrative authority was created. Almost immediately, the state board expressed disappointment in the progress of local health activities. It found that:

> Each city and incorporated village is presumed to have, and certainly should have, a local board of health. Most of them, however, have failed to organize an efficient sanitary system. Very few of the townships, now numbering upwards of 930, maintain boards of health, although a statute providing for such a board has been in existence for thirty years.[2]

Partly as a result of the board's findings, the law requiring the appointment of boards of health and health officers became mandatory for towns in 1885,[3] However, it was not until 1900 that all municipalities had organized health boards. With the reorganization of the state board into a department of health

---

[2] *Ibid.*, p. 68, quoting the *Annual Report of the State Board of Health: 1881.*

[3] Earl W. Murray, "Historical Development of the Public Health Law," *McKinney's Consolidated Laws of New York Annotated,* Vol. 44, p. XXVI.

the following year, the state's organizational structure for health administration in its present form was completed.

A HALF-CENTURY OF INDECISION: STATE VERSUS LOCAL SERVICES

Since 1900, public health in New York State has undergone constant adjustments in the division of responsibility and authority between state and local authorities. Theoretically, the responsibility for public health initially vested in local officials in 1850 has never been removed, but, increasingly, state officials have been forced to perform direct services to supplement minimal local activity. The extension of state services and subsequent attempts to return initiative to local authorities fall into distinguishable periods, highlighted by the reports of two special commissions and the passage of several fundamental statutes.

Strengthening the State Program. By 1913, it had become obvious that merely mandating local health boards into existence would insure neither a uniform nor a high level of local activity. The Governor's Special Health Commission of that year recommended that an expert Public Health Council be attached to the Health Department to develop a state sanitary code. Following the commission's recommendations, the legislature created a council, strengthened the commissioner's administrative powers, and reorganized the State Health Department, redefining its relations with local health boards.

The Public Health Council was authorized to enact a uniform sanitary code to serve as a minimum standard for local compliance. To secure adherence to the code, the Health Commissioner was authorized to "enforce the public health law and the sanitary code" through the "exercise [of] general supervision over the work of all local boards of health and health officers except in the City of New York."[4] The com-

[4] New York, *Laws of 1913*, c. 559 as amended.

missioner was to provide supervision through the sanitary districts into which the state was divided. Originally designed as decentralized supervisory offices of the state department, the sanitary districts soon began conducting inspectional, investigational, and nursing activities for local communities.

The local boards' continued reluctance to undertake more than minimal activities stimulated progressive expansion of services provided by the district offices. Between 1913 and 1920, the state department's expenditures increased from $186,000 to more than 1 million dollars. During this period, the now obvious inadequacies of local organization led to the first attempt to consolidate health units. In 1915, the Public Health Law was amended to enable the formation of consolidated health districts, composed of two or more adjoining health districts. Although consolidation was an alternative available to all health units, the several hundred consolidations that have occurred since 1915 have almost all involved the merger of two or more towns, or a town and a village, into one health unit.

Strengthening Local Organization. In 1921, the state took the first of a number of steps to stimulate the formation of county health departments and to return program initiative to local governments. New York's legislation that authorized boards of supervisors to form county or part-county health districts was part of a nationwide consolidation movement sponsored by the U.S. Public Health Service and the Committee on Administrative Practices of the American Public Health Association.[5] The 1921 legislation prohibited the inclusion of cities of more than 50,000 in the county district. Smaller cities could elect to joint with or remain out of the

---

[5] Onondaga County Department of Research and Development, "Public Health Services in Onondaga County" (mimeographed, August 24, 1956), p. 3.

district. Within a county district, all local boards of health continued to function under the general supervision of the county health board, unless they chose to dissolve themselves or consolidate with others. The county board of supervisors was also empowered to initiate consolidation of local health boards.

To stimulate counties to undertake health programs, a 1923 statute provided matching grants for counties engaging in specific health activities, including hospital construction and operation, nursing, and some general health services. To be eligible for aid, a county was not required to create a county health district, since the aided activities could be conducted by the County Public Health Committee. The latter had neither the powers nor the duties of a county health board but served as the agency for the development of specific health projects. It consisted of representatives of the Board of Supervisors, the medical profession, and laymen.

In addition to the piecemeal grants available to all counties, the state offered to share the costs of a general public-health program, when undertaken by a county health department. This preferential treatment of "organized" counties was the first of a series of financial inducements, intended to stimulate the formation of county districts.

The rural bent of the grant program at this time was revealed by the total exclusion of urban counties from eligibility for state aid. Whether "organized" (in this case only part-county organization would have been possible) or "unorganized" counties containing cities of 50,000 were ineligible for matching state aid.

Thus, by the early 1920's, a number of permissive and stimulative devices were being employed to broaden the bases of local health administration, for the most part with only slight success. Some town and village health consolidations were being undertaken. Permissive legislation providing for the formation of county health districts and departments were largely ignored, until supplemented by the preferential grant program. In 1923, Cattaraugus took advantage of the additional aid available to county health departments. It was the first to form a county health unit. For many years, this rural county received the largest amounts of state aid and conducted one of the state's better local health programs.

Some thought was being given to allowing boards of supervisors to mandate consolidations. However, the passage of even such a relatively forceful measure was not expected to produce adequate results. Commenting on its its probable effectiveness, the Joint Special Committee on Retrenchment and Taxation noted that:

> Under the Public Health Law, town and village authorities have had ample opportunity for several years to consolidate into larger districts. They have not done so. . . . Local political interests are almost invariably against such consolidation. They would continue to be against it even though the board of supervisors of the county, instead of their own town and village boards, were made responsible for affecting consolidation (sic) and political influence can be as readily brought to bear on boards of supervisors as upon town and village boards.[6]

The development of the Joint Committee's thinking reflects the interplay of several economic considerations that invariably accompany proposals for metropolitan action. As its name implied, the committee was motivated by the then current economy-and-efficiency movement. Economy and efficiency usually go hand-in-hand, but they can be applied as completely independent standards. When so used, economy connotes merely a quantitative evaluation of total expenditures. A quali-

[6] State of New York, Joint Special Committee on Taxation and Retrenchment, *1924 Report,* Legislative Document No. 91 (1924) p. 90.

tative as well as quantitative measurement is implied when economy is coupled with efficiency.

The committee adopted a qualitative view of economy, defining it as applying not only to program costs, but also to services received per dollar spent. The committee recommended state-wide adoption of the county department plan, if necessary by legislative mandate. In effect, the committee went on record favoring increased health expenditures, for it realized that:

> If low cost of health administration in New York State is a main objective, no criticism can be made of the present plan. Unquestionably, the consolidation of local health units or the creation of a general health district [by counties] will increase the costs of local services.[7]

Opponents of the county plan appear to have accepted a definition of economy meaning "low cost."

Recognition of the Urban Need. As evidenced by the exclusion of larger cities from county health districts and the disqualification of any counties containing such cities from eligibility for state aid, the intent of the legislation of the early 1920's was to encourage the reorganization and expansion of health activities in rural areas. In a few years, realization of the need for a more positive program of consolidation in both rural and urban areas led to several significant amendments to the Public Health Law.

In 1927, boards of supervisors were given more authority to effect consolidation. The previous protection afforded all local health units in county districts was revoked by empowering the board of supervisors to abolish town boards of health or boards of health of consolidated districts not containing villages. The county agency's responsibility for its territory was further strengthened by subsequent amendments which auto-

[7] *Ibid.*, p. 89.

matically abolished all town boards and village boards in municipalities of less than 3,000, when included in county health districts. While helping to strengthen the county health board, these provisions also served to rally the opponents of the county plan around the flag of localism.

Additional amendments allowed for the optional participation of all cities in county health districts. In 1930, all counties became eligible for state aid. That year marked the end of the state's policy of stimulating only rural county health agencies. By the time of the appointment of the Governor's Special Health Commission of 1930, professional and official opinion overwhelmingly favored more vigorous state leadership in consolidating local health administration.

The commission was appointed by a Governor who had already expressed his dissatisfaction with local government organization and who would later be accused of fostering excessive national centralization as President of the United States. Franklin D. Roosevelt had often commented on the inability of towns and villages to meet the governmental requirements of twentieth-century civilization. He found this nowhere more strikingly apparent than in public health.[8]

The Governor's commission echoed his sentiments. As contrasted with the 1913 commission's emphasis on state policy and organization, the 1930 commission concentrated almost exclusively on local health administration and, in particular, on county health organization. The commission focused attention on the need for metropolitan consolidation and for the first time squarely faced the implications of continued reliance upon the State Department of Health to fill the gaps in local activities. It noted that:

The effort has been made for 18 years to improve town and

---

[8] Governor's Special Health Commission, *Public Health In New York State, op. cit.*, p. 7.

village health administration, but with the exception of added services from the state little improvement has resulted. If local autonomy is to be retained, *no alternative remains except to try a new form of local health organization. . . .*

adding that:

> If the county does not accept the responsibility, the State itself will be obliged to extend its direct health service to meet the health needs of its citizens.[9]

In the boldest proposal to date, the commission recommended the mandatory creation of county health agencies, and the dissolution of all town and village health boards. The commission's suggested reorganization was one of a number of proposals it submitted to the state legislature. Although some of its recommendations were enacted into legislation, the county-health-unit plan was shelved. Almost fifteen years elapsed before the legislature again seriously considered the role of the county in health administration.

THE FRUIT OF INDECISION

By 1946, only six counties had organized health departments: Cattaraugus, 1923; Cortland, 1929; Columbia, 1932; Suffolk, 1938; Westchester, 1929; Nassau, 1938. Four of these early "organized" counties were predominantly rural, and only Westchester contained any cities of considerable size. At its inception, the Westchester Health District included none of the county's cities. Its several villages of more than 3,000 retained their local health boards. Subsequently most of the villages elected to dissolve their local boards, and one city joined the county district; but for many years Westchester was pointed to as exemplifying the difficulty of integrating county operations while retaining local health boards.[10]

---

[9] *Ibid.*, pp. 98 and 132 (italicized in the original).

[10] State of New York, Commission to Formulate a Long Range Health Program, *Interim Report*, Legislative Document No. 83 (1941), p. 188.

Interestingly, three of the early "organized" counties were associated with a single metropolitan area, New York City. None of the upstate metropolitan counties had elected to form health agencies. The action of the counties bordering New York City is partly explained by conditions endemic to that area. The closeness of the very active New York City Health Department, the service-level expectations of city migrants to the outlying counties, indications that the medical associations of Westchester, Nassau, and Suffolk were more vocal in their support of county health boards than their upstate counterparts, all help to explain differences in upstate and downstate behavior. Upstate counties appear to have been more influenced by other factors that to this day tend to delay acceptance of health consolidation.

State Activities and County Health Organization. Although the State Health Department had an announced policy of encouraging the formation of county health districts, its actions partly contradicted its intentions. Faced with increasing evidence of the need for more services, the department subordinated organizational goals to the expediency of securing more health services from whatever source.

The continued extension of direct state services resulted from the repeated triumph of program demands over organizational ideals. State officials were cognizant of the counter-impact their services had upon the policy of stimulating county-health-unit formation. The more services the state provided, the less evident was the need for local action. Under political, ideological, and fiscal conditions that precluded centralized administration of a comprehensive health program from Albany, state officials were forced to wait for local need to become sufficiently apparent to produce local action or to extend their own activities, knowing that their capacity for action would necessarily be limited. Professional and moral considerations argued against waiting.

In addition to providing more services, the department and the legislature helped bolster opposition to county consolidation by supporting the development of piecemeal health programs and by extending grants-in-aid to unorganized counties. Through their Public Health Committees, counties were authorized to undertake many activities normally included in a health department's program. Although the "unorganized" county lacked the powers and personnel deemed necessary for a complete health program, the Department of Health supported the development of piecemeal county activities as a means of, at least partially, filling observable needs, fully realizing that the availability of technical guidance from district officers and grants-in-aid from Albany would dull much of the incentive for county-department formation.

Finances and County Health Organization. A further obstacle to county district formation has been its impact on county tax sources. This has been particularly important in the upstate metropolitan counties, where large central cities constitute the greater part of the county's tax base. Under the "unorganized" system, health programs were a general county charge supported by county-wide taxes, despite the fact that services were usually supplied only to non-city residents. If cities elected to remain outside of "organized" county districts, however, their property was no longer available for taxation in support of the county health programs. Rural county leaders have preferred not to organize a county district and risk the chance of losing the city tax bases. This was one of the factors later influencing state officials to press for full-county, as opposed to part-county, health districts. It also inspired the 1932 commission to recommend that cities be taxed for support of a county health district, regardless of whether they were a part of it.[11]

Financial considerations also account for the state legislature's failure to take any decisive action regarding local organization. The 1930's were difficult years; even the Health Department's county promotional program was realistically suspended due to local financial incapacity. The legislature's reluctance to continue to press for county organization is understandable in the light of potential grant costs to the state, if all counties were to become "organized." In 1936 it was estimated that annual grants would total 3½ million dollars, if all counties were to form health departments, as opposed to 1 million dollars, if the counties were to take maximum advantage of the Public Health Committee system.[12] The difference in potential cost to the state is undoubtedly much larger today.

Local Deterrents to County Health Organization. The several deterrents to county organization already described were largely built into legislative and departmental policies and were motivated by earlier desires to stimulate public-health activities, regardless of their effect upon the state's ultimate objective of forming county health departments. State policies have since been altered to bring departmental action into accord with that objective; but some obstacles to the county plan are largely beyond the state's capacity to control. One such is the resistance displayed by hundreds of part-time local health officers to any proposal that promises to make their job obsolete. The provision abolishing town and village health boards and health-officer positions in the law authorizing county health departments is credited with contributing most

---

[11] Governor's Special Health Commission, *Public Health in New York State, op. cit.*, p. 101

[12] Commission on State Aid to Municipal Subdivision, *Report, op. cit.*, p. 329.

of the opposition to health consolidation prior to 1945.[13] Local health officers are still a major source of opposition, even though considerable concessions were given to them in the 1946 revision of the Public Health Law.

THE 1946 PUBLIC-HEALTH LAW

The 1946 amendments to the Public Health Law represented total legislative and departmental commitment to the promotion of county health departments. Through one revision, the legislature attempted to soften local health officers' resistance. It permitted the retention of all local health boards and officers within a county district. This seeming regression sacrificed some of the potential efficiency of the county department to the more immediate end of getting the departments established. However, the department assumed, correctly as subsequent events proved, that the retention of local health officers would usually last only as long as the interest and practice of incumbent officials.

A second, and equally important, revision was the additional inducement offered to county health departments in the form of larger grants-in-aid. "Organized" counties were singled out for a reimbursement of 75 per cent of the first $100,000 expended and 50 per cent of expenditures in excess of $100,000. "Unorganized" counties retained their eligibility for 50 per cent reimbursement; but the differential was apparently sufficient to immediately induce the formation of county departments in Schoharie, Rensselaer, and Ulster.

A new feature of the 1946 legislation was the provision of a 50 per cent grant for health activities in cities of more than 50,000. This legislative maneuver coincided with mounting city displeasure with the state-aid program recommended by the Moore Commission. Accusations that a rural-dominated

---

[13] Onondaga County Department of Research and Development, "Public Health Services in Onondaga County," *op. cit.*, p. 5.

Republican legislature was short-changing urban areas led to the inclusion of the large cities in the health-grant program. New York City and the Westchester cities were particularly affected by the new grant, since the former was precluded from eligibility for county grants and the latter had previously elected to remain out of the Westchester county health district.

At first glance it may appear that grants to cities effectively removed one of the major inducements for cities to join county districts. Certainly, without state grants the Westchester cities would probably not have continued to remain out of the county district or at least would have refrained from expanding their own programs. This would probably also have been true of upstate metropolitan cities. But in 1946 the State Health Department would have been very satisfied if all counties containing larger cities had formed part-county departments, especially if at the same time the grants would stimulate cities to increase their services.

In general, the availability of grants to cities has not appeared to offset seriously the advantages of city-county consolidation of health services. Health officials and political leaders in Albany, Troy, Buffalo, Rochester, and Syracuse have all supported the merger of their city departments with their respective counties. Although grants to cities eliminated what might have been a compulsion for merger, they do not seem to have encouraged cities to "go it alone."

THE COUNTY HEALTH DEPARTMENTS

In 1946, the State Health Department viewed the grant system as the core of its efforts to return responsibility for public health to counties and cities and to withdraw from direct program operation. Anticipating the formation of county departments, the state reorganized its field system in 1948. Five regional offices were created to serve as the link between the state department and local officials. District offices were retained on a par with local agencies. They would continue to provide direct services and supervision to unorganized counties but were not to function in organized counties or cities. Eventually, district offices would be abandoned as all counties and cities developed their health departments.

The 1946 legislation provoked an immediate increase in the number of county departments. City health programs were also notably expanded through the stimulation of state grants. But the formation of county districts later slackened and anticipation of early attainment of the department's objectives is not great. In 1960, there were twenty county departments.

Table 3. County Health Departments, When Created

Cattaraugus	1923	Schoharie	1946	Clinton	1953
Suffolk	1928	Ulster	1946	Genesee	1953
Cortland	1929	Erie	1947	Rockland	1957
Westchester	1929	Tompkins	1947	Dutchess	1957
Columbia	1932	Albany	1949	Chemung	1958
Nassau	1938	Seneca	1949	Monroe	1959
Rensselaer	1946	Wyoming	1951		

SOURCE: State of New York, Department of Health, *Annual Reports*.

The accompanying map indicates the counties that have formed departments and the metropolitan counties of the state. The instances of consolidation do not reveal any truly consistent pattern. The departments are relatively well distributed, though with a heavy concentration around New York City. Of the thirteen upstate metropolitan counties, only four have adopted the county plan. These four departments, however, serve the central cities of Buffalo, Rochester, Albany, and Troy.

There is a noticable absence of county organizations in the central area surrounding the Syracuse and Utica-Rome metropolitan areas. This absence, extending as far as recently organized Monroe, when contrasted with the clustering of county

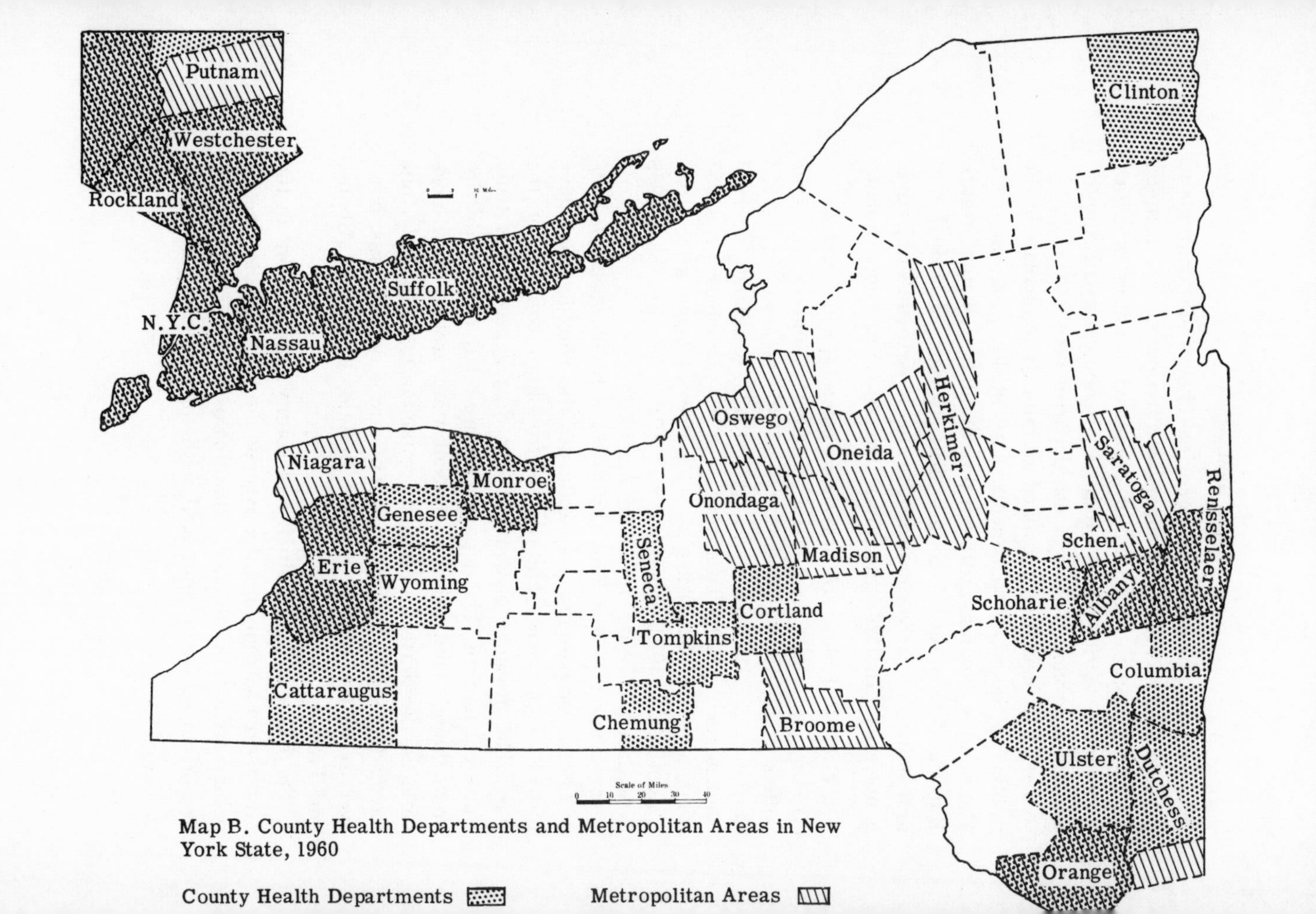

Map B. County Health Departments and Metropolitan Areas in New York State, 1960

departments around the Buffalo and Albany areas, suggests that the action of less urban counties may follow examples set by neighboring urban centers. An interesting inference, but who followed whom at Albany, and what explains Clinton's and Chemung's decision?

More than likely, the propensity to initiate consolidation is more dependent upon unique local conditions than upon any general characteristics attributable to urban or non-urban areas. The impact and effectiveness of the state's stimulative program is similarly conditioned by local factors largely independent of state influence.

Grants-in-aid appear to have been a more decisive influence in the rural counties, where $100,000 substantially supports the entire health program. In the more populous counties, the enticement of state funds has been tempered by realization that a county program would require additional local expenditures far greater than those now made for minimal services. With the state partially reimbursing "unorganized" counties, the stimulus for county organization must stem principally from other than financial considerations. The consistent support for county departments from city officials indicates that professional opinion is one significant motivation.

The state's promotional campaign has reflected the variable impact of the grant program. Following the 1946 amendments, the department surveyed health activities in more than twenty unorganized counties. Public information pamphlets were distributed in each county, describing the anticipated advantages of a county department. Although service benefits and increased aid were discussed in all the pamphlets, the emphasis placed upon financial inducements varied directly with the urbanism of the counties. In contrast to its appeal to rural counties to get more service from state money, the Health Department dealt with Onondaga County by pointing to its metropolitan health needs, incidentally reminding its residents that state funds would help defray part of the anticipated increased expenditures.[14]

Financial considerations other than grants-in-aid have significantly contributed to consolidation in some urban areas. The county health department provided political leaders of Buffalo with a convenient method of relieving the city's financial difficulties. Dangerously close to its property tax limit, Buffalo gained some breathing room by transferring expenditures for health services from the city's budget to the county.

In Onondaga County, supervisors from city wards are currently resentful of the mounting expenditures for county health programs from which the city derives no direct benefits. The Majority Leader of the Board of Supervisors, a city supervisor, is reported to have refused to support further increases in the county health budget. Faced with a growing population that will undoubtedly result in an increase in service demands, the county will thus either be forced to create a county or part-county department, or rely on local boards of health to expand their activities. But local boards are not eligible for grants.

Financial pressures are felt in more than one way. In a study of public-health facilities in Onondaga County, A. W. Olson conservatively estimated city residents would save $60,000 by joining a county health district. A county department would cost non-city residents an additional $15,000 for the much higher level of services they could expect to receive.[15] The costs

[14] The differing bases of appeal are strikingly evident in comparing the pamphlets distributed in Onondaga County and Livingston or Franklin Counties. *See* State of New York, Department of Health, *Public Health Services for Livingston County* (n. d.); *Public Health Services for Franklin County* (n. d.); *Public Health Services for Onondaga County* (n. d.).

[15] Alvin Walter Olson, "Some Aspects of Functional Consolidation in Public Health Services—With Special Reference to Onondaga County, New York" (unpublished D.S.S. dissertation, Syracuse University, August, 1956), pp. 247–277.

were estimated on the basis of county-wide health expenditure of $3 per capita. The State Health Department arrived at a similar conclusion using a different method.[16]

Both Mr. Olson and the department failed to take into account the period of transition during which the county program is increased to equal that of the city or, in Mr. Olson's terms, that period in which per capita expenditures for county residents are raised to equal the city level. It is quite reasonable to assume that most of the county department's attention and resources would be devoted to non-city areas during this period, and that city residents might justifiably feel their interinterests were being neglected.

The problem of equalizing services is a recognized hindrance to metropolitan activity. In the health field, it has been particularly significant in Broome County. Binghamton and the populous villages of Endicott and Johnson City have not been willing to work through a county agency. Perhaps these three urban jurisdictions present service-level difficulties too complex to be resolved voluntarily. Certainly Syracuse and Rochester have felt more is to be gained than lost through consolidation, although the former's citizens have yet to convince their county neighbors.

FUTURE STATE POLICY

The Commissioner of Health of New York State has announced his intention to encourage, but not attempt to force, county health department formation. He insists that action must voluntarily follow local initiative. Some of his subordinates are equally insistent that more positive state action is necessary. They have suggested that the grant-in-aid be used as a more flexible means of stimulation. Grant requirements are flexible enough, they believe, for the commissioner to refuse to

[16] State Department of Health, *Public Health Services for Onondaga County, op. cit.*, pp. 32–33.

reimburse some "unorganized" activities, while suggesting that such programs would be reimbursable if conducted by a county department. Although the commissioner is hesitant to gamble with local authorities, to some extent this method is now being employed on a discretionary basis by regional directors. They have, on occasion, individually applied a standard of effectiveness of general health services in evaluating unorganized county requests for reimbursement.

In several other ways, the department is doing more than merely waiting for local initiative to develop. In a negative sense, it is promoting county formation by consciously refusing to expand the staff and services of district offices. The department has also stopped encouraging counties to undertake piecemeal programs. Political and professional pressures are great, but the department is gambling that county departments will be created before the lack of services becomes too serious a problem.

In a positive vein, the department is attempting to minimize part-time, local health officers' resistance to consolidation. It has developed a plan for absorbing local health officers as deputies to the county health officer, the deputies receiving their fees for services from the county. Thus incumbents may retain the economic and social advantages now gained by their identification as public health officials, without greatly endangering the program of the county department. This identification is apparently highly regarded by the physicians who serve as part-time, local health officers in most local health units.

Despite all the state's efforts to create conditions favorable to the formation of county departments, consolidation is still completely dependent upon local acceptance. To influence local opinion, the State Health Department conducts an intensive public information and educational campaign. Personal and professional contacts are maintained with local and state organizations active in the health field. These and other social agencies and community organizations are valuable "resources" upon whom the state department depends for local leadership. Influencing and convincing their leaders are major tasks of the regional and district officers.

CONCLUSION

Although the state has what may be considered a metropolitan objective in health administration, its ability to complete a transition to county health departments has been weakened by its own past actions. Health administration has suffered from overexperimentation in organizational alternatives. The availability of services from the state, local, and county offices and the often conflicting incentives the state has offered for alternative local actions have produced loyalties to programs that only partially fulfill health needs and have created unwarranted local confidence in the adequacy of existing programs.

Although the state has attempted to promote the formation of county health units, it has historically supported other forms of organization at the same time. As in the case of water-pollution control, short-range objectives have always triumphed over long-range goals.

As the state's major tool of influence, the grant-in-aid has not provided sufficient economic motivation for health consolidation. The state has not been able to resist pressures to support local health services, regardless of the type of agency performing them. The original grant, "conditional" upon the formation of county districts, was supplanted with categorical grants for specific services provided by Public Health Committees and, after 1946, with grants to cities that were poorly disguised measures of tax relief. Consequently, with money available to them from several sources, the added incentives for county organization have not offered enough extra compensation for local leaders to challenge existing, politically satisfactory health arrangements.

The county health issue rarely advances beyond political and professional consideration. The health issue is not as dramatic or as obvious as transportation or water supply. It rarely arouses public concern and is generally resolved by the interplay of professional and political organizations. Where the consolidation movement has succeeded, much of its momentum can be traced to the State Health Department's early efforts to convince and gain the support of political, professional, and volunteer organizations.

Grant incentives have played only a minor role in achieving consolidations. Many would have been undertaken purely in recognition of the superiority of the county form of organization. Health services were transferred to Erie County for financial reasons other than grant assistance. The State Health Department has been criticized for overemphasizing financial benefits in its promotional campaigns. Critics contend that the county plan has been adopted where need has been demonstrated. They urge the department to concentrate on convincing the public and its leaders that the county plan merits support, not for financial, but for program reasons.

The Health Department takes a more pessimistic view of local political conditions. In its review of local programs, it finds little evidence that the initiation or continued support of county health programs is inspired by popular desires to better community health. The department is frankly disappointed in a number of its local counterparts. Yet it continues to strive for further decentralization of its own authority, even where, as in subdivision control, decentralization may lead to local relaxation of standards.

The literature of public health provides the reason for the

state's attitude. Few other fields of writing display as much preoccupation with grass-roots ideology and local control. In public health, decentralization is more than a slogan, it is a conviction. A public-health program contains elements of regulation, education, and service. Public participation and cooperation are required in each program component. Local control offers greater opportunity for health officials to gain the public confidence and cooperation required for their work.

Experience with state control of subdivisions has revealed the great lengths to which subdividers and local officers will go to circumvent requirements imposed upon them. Although decentralization may subject local officials to overwhelming pressures to lower standards, the educational value stemming from the local promulgation and enforcement of standards may have a salutary effect on the future of the regulatory program. In effect, state officials believe it is better to have acceptance of lesser standards than connivance to undermine more restrictive standards.

Mandating county health departments into existence will never create the local conditions that health officials deem desirable for the conduct of a community health program. The grant-in-aid certainly does little to foster health consciousness or other positive public-health attitudes. Where need is recognized, good public-health programs are possible. In part, the state has been unable to convince localities of the need for an area-wide organization for health services, because of its past success in providing and fostering local, minimal services. Ironically, the department's present policy of stimulating local demand by restricting its own district-office activities has caused it to refrain from employing health educators at the district level. Yet the local activities of just such persons might be the most successful means of stimulating popular awareness of the need for county health organization.

V

Public Education

One of the more formidable obstacles to the efficiency of our common schools is believed to be unnecessary multiplication and subdivision of districts. In those portions of the state where the population is scattered over a large extent of territory, the convenience and accommodation of the inhabitants require the formation of districts comprising a small amount of taxable territory applicable to the support of schools and a limited number of children. But where an opposite state of things exists the interests of education will be most effectively promoted by assigning to each district the greatest extent of territory compatible with securing to the children the requisite facilities for their regular attendance at schools.[1]

Reworded in the more familiar reporting style of modern educators, the above analysis of one of the most vexing problems of public education could well have been written by any of a number of contemporary state education directors. And with the elimination of some specific references to education it might be construed as a general description of today's metropolitan problem. However, it was written in 1853, long before international scientific competition had touched off contem-

[1] *Annual Report of the Superintendent of Education: 1853,* quoted in A. G. Grace and G. A. Moe, *State Aid and School Costs (The Regents Inquiry)* (New York: McGraw-Hill Book Co., 1938), p. 23.

porary concern for the adequacy of American education and long before there was anything called a metropolitan problem in New York.

If the metropolitan problem is nothing more than the task of providing services economically and democratically, then Superintendent Young's statement might be cited to support the contention that metropolitan problems are neither new nor limited to the more urban areas of the state. For more than a century, public education has exemplified the difficulty of providing a governmental service through the mechanism of a multitude of governmental units. But the intensity of the metropolitan problem is more than a reflection of the number of units of local government. The movement for consolidation of school districts has been relatively successful in New York. Yet the reduction of the number of school districts has had little effect on the integration of governmental policy, particularly fiscal policy, in metropolitan areas.

The competition for resources and for public support among governmental programs in metropolitan areas is not found in less-urban places. The complexities of urbanism place the problems of education within a wider context of political action. Expanded and professionalized, the school district becomes just one of a number of governmental units, seemingly racing to reach their debt and tax limitations and competing with each other for tax resources in the process. Population in metropolitan areas is nearly as diversified and dispersed as in the central city, resulting in a uniformity of needs and of expectations that those needs will be met. Concurrent planning for school growth is an acknowledged necessity but, in the light of multiple and competing school districts, is as difficult to achieve as metropolitan planning itself. The impact of the metropolitan environment challenges the capability of the traditional methods of educational policy formulation: the school board, and the district voter meeting.

In 1853, Superintendent Young recognized the differences confronting the organization, conduct, and financing of public education in the state's urban and rural areas. The rural challenge provoked the movement for rural centralization, subsequently extended to urban areas. In the process, however, the unique problems of urban education have been virtually ignored. Until very recently, educational leaders seem to have been exclusively concerned with the problem of the one-room rural school.

THE EDUCATION SYSTEM

Responsibility for public education is presently shared by the state government and local communities organized into school districts. That the division of responsibilities is neither static nor clearly defined is repeatedly illustrated by local complaints over state policy requirements and by state efforts to convince local districts that the responsibility for raising school revenue is theirs, not Albany's. One thing is certain. Home rule does not apply to education, despite district complains about state "interference." Education is a state function. Although locally elected, school-board members are state officials. This chief factor, legally distinguishing education from other local functions, supports the contention that education is unique and must be treated differently from other governmental activities locally undertaken.

Except for the "big six"—New York, Buffalo, Rochester, Syracuse, Albany, and Yonkers—every school district in New York State is an independent unit of government. The school boards of the "big six" are financially dependent upon city authorities. All others are free to determine their own financial policies, subject, however, to more direct voter participation in the budgetary process than is characteristic of other governmental units.

The state has increasingly been called upon to provide financial aid to local districts. Indeed, the history of state grants in New York begins with education. Educational grants have been used for all the objectives of which this device is capable. It was by means of grants that the state was able to assume control of local school practices and to institute statewide, free public education in the mid-nineteenth century.[2] The announced intention of the grant system today is to provide equalization and a minimum level of education to all students. Although state grants for education are still somewhat conditional, the bickering and bargaining that accompanied the distribution of additional funds in 1960 leaves the distinct impression that local officials regard the grants as a matter of right and as a form of tax relief, justified by the fact that education is, after all, a state function.

The basis of state participation in educational finance is the foundation program. The foundation program represents a minimum expenditure per child by the state. It consists of a combination of state and local contributions that operates to equalize differences in district wealth. Each district is required to levy a uniform minimum real estate tax in support of its program. The differences between the amount thus raised and the total foundation program constitutes the state contribution, or the equalization quota. Thus wealthier districts contribute more and receive proportionately less state funds than poorer districts. All districts may spend in excess of their foundation

[2] Harold L. Rakov, "The Political Orientation of the Public School as Reflected in the Evolution and Present Structure of the New York State Public School System" (unpublished Ph.D. dissertation, Syracuse University, 1955), Chap. III, "The Institutionalization of the New York Public School."

programs, while retaining eligibility for their equalization quotas. Most do.

The basic foundation formula is augmented by a number of computations that take into account such factors as rapid growth, small size, incentives for centralization, and protection from loss of revenue due to subsequent formula changes. In addition, supplemental grants are available for transportation, school construction (annually for central schools, on an emergency basis for others) and special classes.

To protect districts from losing money as a result of formula revisions, minimum state flat grants have been awarded to all districts affected by a formula change. The minimum usually freezes into the aid formula relationships that existed in past years and are not expected to occur again. Although several have noted that the flat grant is non-equalizing, no group given the task of revising the aid formula has ever dared suggest its discontinuance.[3]

FACTORS AFFECTING SCHOOL-DISTRICT SIZE

When speaking of school-district organization, it is well to keep in mind the distinction between an administrative unit and an attendance unit. An attendance unit comprises the area served by a single school. It does not necessarily constitute a taxing unit, nor does it have an independent system of administration. An administrative unit is that area supporting and administering an educational program. It decides educational policy within the limits allowed it by a central authority.

It is possible to design an educational system so as to make an administrative unit conform to an attendance unit. The boundaries of the district and the financial resources available

---

[3] *See* the treatment given the flat grant by the most recent study commission, State of New York, Temporary Commission on Educational Finances, *Financing Public Education in New York State* (Albany: 1956), p. 32.

to it are thus limited by students' eligibility to attend one school. This was the organizational pattern characteristic of New York's common school districts, prior to the advent of modern transportation and the state policy of encouraging consolidation. On the other hand, it is possible to include a number of attendance units within one administrative unit. This is the structure characteristic of city schools. The city school district usually includes a number of elementary and secondary school attendance units integrated into a comprehensive educational program offering specialized classes and facilities that might not be practical for one attendance unit alone.

Pupil Population. The importance of the size of the administrative unit is commensurate with both its ability to support an educational program and the quality of that program. The inability of the one-room, one-teacher school to provide a progressive, stimulating learning experience for advancing grade-school students has long been a problem in rural areas. The provision of specialized instruction is hardly possible until the school's pupil population is large enough to warrant division into separate learning categories. At the secondary level, the investment in plant and equipment required for technical or vocational offerings necessitates an assurance of pupil demand that few but the larger cities of the state can now afford.

Estimates of the pupil population required to take advantage of the benefits of instructional specialization are continually increasing. In 1938, it was estimated that a satisfactory program could be offered only if the unit served not less than 1,200 pupils in kindergarten through twelfth grade. By 1956, this minimum had been revised to 1,700, and no grade school, regardless of size, was considered adequate unless it formed part of a high-school district.[4] Today, the State Education

[4] The classic work on district size is Howard A. Dawson, *Satisfactory*

Department favors the creation of districts composed of no fewer than 2,500 pupils.

The upward revision of population standards is the result partly of the continued specialization of curriculum and partly of the increased ease of modern transportation. In 1853, Superintendent Young had to concede that convenience required the existence of many small school districts in less populous areas, but today the ease of transportation has greatly reduced the applicability of even this exception. Nevertheless, there are still many districts in urban as well as rural areas that fail to meet even the earlier standards.

Financial Capacity. Instructional content is also affected by a district's financial capacity. In the long run, financial limits, represented either by a lack of tax sources or an unwillingness to employ them, act as a ceiling beyond which further stimulation for program improvement will have little effect. The economic resources available to a district are often directly related to the amount of territory within its jurisdiction. Consolidation and enlargement of school districts is thus doubly motivated. Increased size, reflected in larger enrollments, offers greater opportunity for curriculum specialization, and it also affords the district a broader revenue base.

To some extent, the creation of larger administrative units also produces an equalizing effect. Although the Commissioner of Education and the courts have ruled that equalization in its own right is a legitimate end of redistricting,[5] this purpose has largely been subsidiary to considerations of pupil size. However, the changed relationships of district wealth resulting from

---

School Districts (Nashville: Division of Surveys and Field Studies, George Peabody College for Teachers, 1934). The development of New York's standards are traced in Temporary Commission on Educational Finances, *Financing Public Education in New York State, op. cit.*, p. 233.

[5] *McKinney's Consolidated Laws of New York Annotated,* Vol. 16, p. 510.

redistricting has been one of the greatest impediments to local acceptance of centralization.

Increasing a district's size does not always increase its financial capacity. Up to a point (usually when additional construction becomes necessary), economies of scale will produce a relative increase in wealth as district size increases, even though the per pupil resources brought to the district are less than those previously enjoyed. Beyond this point, it is financially advantageous for a district to increase its size only if the students added bring with them tax assessables equal to or greater than those possessed by students already in attendance. If they do not, increases in size then become locally desirable only in terms of instructional gains and not economic advantages. The state's need to offer financial inducements for centralization testifies, unfortunately, to the local priority of values.

In New York and in most other states, wealth is usually measured in terms of the value of property subject to taxation. Realistically, measurements of financial capacity must also include a qualitative evaluation of propensities to tax. In an early state education grant, districts were rewarded for greater tax efforts. This provision was later abandoned as contrary to the principle of equalization. The present requirement of a uniform local contribution to the foundation program is, however, a continuation of efforts to require a minimum, uniform local tax effort. Wealth to be equalized is that portion of local resources available after the minimum effort has been made.

Although some consideration of effort does enter into the equalization formula, it fails to take into account any other governmental programs supported by residents of the school district. A $10 tax rate for two school districts may represent entirely different degrees of effort, depending upon the cumulative demands of other taxing units. No school district enjoys the exclusive right to tax property within its boundaries. Few operate within the same totality of governmental activity. Significantly, the current "taxpayers revolt" has also been labeled a "suburban revolt." The extensive demands and outlays for government services in suburban areas truly present a challenge to community effort.

No equalization grant program in New York or elsewhere has ever considered the simultaneous use of the real estate tax by several governmental units as a factor in measuring financial capacity. That it is an important determinant of expenditures is evidenced by the grant of fiscal independence to city schools in 1951 and by continued efforts to win independence for the "big six." Indeed, without similar independent authority to raise revenues, it becomes impossible to compare the fiscal efforts of the "big six" and other school districts. While comparisons can be made among independent districts, they too are far from realistic, measuring, as they do, expenditures for education alone.

Although primarily defended on other grounds, the movement for fiscal independence is partly motivated by a desire to remove education from direct political competition for economic resources. With a path cleared to community sentiment, educators hope to stimulate a high level of tax effort for educational purposes, irrespective of the financial needs of other governmental activities. Stimulation takes the form of repeated assertion of the importance and uniqueness of education and in a concentrated effort to foster an intense school-citizen identity, through formal association of the citizen with the school system.

Relating the school to the community it served was an early reason for pursuing citizen-school identification. Today, less lofty reasons motivate efforts to bring citizens closer to their schools. Commissioner of Education Allen favors increasing citizen contact and participation as a means of stimulating greater tax effort. Allen feels taxpayers revolt only when they are not involved in levying the taxes themselves (a new version of "taxation without representation . . ."). If people would take an interest in their school, they would be only too glad to increase taxes.[6]

Fostering strong attachments to existing school districts, however, bolsters opposition to centralization, which the commissioner also feels is necessary. Community-school identity is today based upon narrowly drawn community boundaries. The school district itself creates a community. Unfortunately, its area is too small to maximize educational or financial capacity. Not that the centralization movement seeks a truly realistic redefinition of boundaries. Until now it has been based purely upon pupil-population standards. The state has made little effort to encourage centralizations beyond the size necessary to embrace the number of pupils considered adequate for a general educational offering.

THE CENTRALIZATION MOVEMENT

The term *centralization* has two educational usages. It refers to the progressive reduction of numbers of school districts and, in a more technical sense, to a particular method of reduction—the creation of central school districts. In addition to the formation of central districts, reductions may be accomplished through consolidation, annexation, and the general redefinition of district boundaries. The several forms of enlarged districts differ primarily in regard to their financial relationships with the state and their methods of creation.

Although there were nineteenth-century antecedents, as a planned public policy, centralization is decidedly a twentieth-

[6] *New York Times,* March 9, 1959, p. 7.

century occurrence. State education authorities have often been criticized for not being active enough in developing new programs and curricula, but the success of centralization is generally acknowledged to be due to the positive role they have played in reorganization.[7] The consolidation of city school districts in 1904, followed by the Consolidated School District Act of 1913 and the Central Rural School District Act of 1914, provided the initial authorization and impetus for state-wide reduction in the number of school districts.

The earliest economic stimulant to consolidation was the provision of the Union Free School Act of 1853, guaranteeing the common school districts that were merging into a union free district all the aid to which they were previously entitled, for five more years. The state has since continued the practice of offering financial inducements to centralization. Until very recently, central districts received a bonus 12 per cent correction of their foundation programs. Today's incentives consist of additional aid for construction and transportation. They were originally designed to compensate for higher costs incurred by rural central districts. Today, central districts continue to receive preferential treatment, not in recognition of higher costs, but as an admitted incentive for centralization.

The philosophy motivating central-district incentives has been stated and reiterated by the State Education Department and every legislative committee and special commission that has studied public education. It stresses the positive nature of financial incentives as opposed to negative penalties for failure to centralize. Incentives have been added to existing grants, despite the fact that the basic grants may help retain small and inefficient districts; for it is easier for the State Edu-

---

[7] State of New York, Temporary Commission on the Revision and Simplification of the Constitution, "Education," *Staff Report No. 26* (mimeographed, n.d.) p. 72.

cation Department to recommend and for the legislature to enact a measure increasing grants to central districts than one reducing benefits for small, inefficient units. The fate of the Heald Commission's proposal to modify the small school correction is illustrative.

The appointment of the Heald Commission (Temporary Commission on Educational Finances) in 1954 was necessitated by a change in the state equalization ratios. The changed relationships of property values threatened drastically to reduce total amounts of state aid and to upset the equalization quotas of the foundation formula. The commission was authorized to survey educational finances and organization comprehensively and to propose adjustments in the formula.

The commission reaffirmed the policy of promoting centralization through positive incentives and frankly urged continuation of preferential treatment for central districts, not because of their higher costs, but as a stimulant to further centralization. However, several of its recommendations were virtually punitive in their impact upon districts not participating in centralization.

The commission recommended retraction of tuition allowances paid by the state to contracting districts—those not operating schools, but transporting pupils to other districts. It also suggested a change in the central district, small school correction computed as part of the foundation program. The small central school correction had been added to the 12 per cent central school bonus. In order to promote the further centralization of smaller central schools, the commission recommended separation of the two corrections. A small school correction would be made available to all schools, *provided they were not scheduled for centralization under the state's Master Plan,* and only larger central districts would continue to receive the 12 per cent central school correction. To reinforce these changes, the commission proposed to exclude small districts and contracting districts from the protection of the "save harmless" clause, guaranteeing districts minimum foundation aid, totaling 110 per cent of their 1955/56 apportionments.[8]

The State Education Department and the legislature accepted almost all of the Heald Commission's recommendations but balked at enacting the punitive measures. In an affirmation of the policy of stimulation through positive not negative action, the "save harmless" clause was revised to guarantee 110 per cent apportionment to all districts.[9]

The Centralization Procedure. Similar examples of legislative and executive reluctance to pressure school districts into centralization are provided by the history of the Master Plan and by the procedures through which centralization is effected. Although education is a state function, the cry of home rule has often been raised to demand less state interference in local district activity. In 1917, the legislature went so far as to abolish all school districts, replacing them with a township system of organization. Only one town attempted and succeeded in fulfilling the transition. As the result of widespread rural opposition, the legislation was repealed.[10] Since then, little serious consideration has been given to securing reorganization through mandate.

As in most aspects of education, centralization is put into motion through a combination of state and local action. The fine distinctions between consolidation, annexation, and

---

[8] Temporary Commission on Educational Finances, *Financing Public Education in New York State, op. cit.,* pp. 16–17.

[9] New York, *Laws of 1957,* c. 982. *See* the supporting memorandum of the Education Department in *New York State Legislative Annual: 1957,* p. 534.

[10] Harlan Hoyt Homer, *Education in New York: 1784–1954* (Albany: University of the State of New York, State Education Department, 1954), p. 49.

centralization are nowhere more evident than in the procedures by which they are put into effect. All three may be initiated by local petition, and in the final analysis each is contingent upon local approval, but the timing and effectiveness of state or local action vary.

A central district may be formed only by the Commissioner of Education and only with the approval of the qualified school voters in the proposed district. A district superintendent (the local representative of the Education Department) may order a consolidation or annexation of districts within his supervisory district. His order is final unless challenged by a petition. If challenged, the superintendent's order must be approved by local vote prior to going into effect. In practice, however, redistricting is almost always locally initiated. State officials rarely chance having an order challenged and voted down, although they do encourage local citizen groups to prepare communities for centralization procedures.

The Master Plan. The proposed boundaries of a central district must be laid out by the commissioner prior to the centralization election. In laying out districts, the commissioner generally adheres to the Master Plan for District Reorganization, developed in 1947 and revised to date. The Master Plan now calls for only 500 districts in the state. It is, however, only a guide.

The Master Plan is the outgrowth of the 1938 Regents Inquiry Into the Nature and Costs of Education. Much of the Inquiry's study concerned district organization and finance. The staff report on state aid to education suggested that a master plan for 800 districts be prepared. It described in detail the types of districts to be created. There was to be a clear rural-urban separation of schools. City districts and village independencies would cover the urban areas, while the rest of the state was to be served by central districts. In an interesting sidelight, the staff rejected the possibility of using the county as a basis for organizing non-urban territory, noting that, since counties were not exactly models of good government, at this time "no sound argument can be made for attaching the school system to an unsound base."[11]

In his summary of the inquiry findings, Luther Gulick did not touch upon the nature of the needed reorganization, but he did repeat his staff's suggestion that a special commission be appointed to prepare a master plan. He also agreed that the final plan be mandated by the legislature. But Gulick and his staff appeared to differ significantly in the general role they assigned to the State Education Department. The staff report had described the conflicting opinions within the State Education Department regarding the Commission's need for coercive powers and seemed to side with those favoring more power for the department. Gulick recommended as an operating concept enlightened professional, non-coercive state leadership.[12]

The State Education Department placed a one-year moratorium on new central districts, while waiting for legislative action. But the legislature found the inquiry's recommendations for a mandatory districting plan "objectionable."[13] It appointed a legislative committee to develop a Master Plan, stipulating that the plan be used as a guide. Developed between 1943 and 1947, the since revised Master Plan for District Reorganization still serves as the basis for local reorganization.

Lacking authority to effect centralizations in accordance with the plan and apparently unwilling to press the legislature

[11] Grace and Moe, *op. cit.*, pp. 240–241.

[12] Luther Gulick, *Education for American Life: The Regents Inquiry* (New York: McGraw-Hill Book Co., 1938), pp. 64–65.

[13] "The plan offered by the Regent's Inquiry was never taken seriously since it contained a number of objectionable features." State of New York, Joint Legislative Committee on the State Educational System, *Master Plan for School District Reorganization,* Legislative Document No. 25 (1947), p. 12.

to mandate centralization, the State Education Department must wait for local districts to request centralization. Experience in New York and throughout the country offers little evidence that localities desire to initiate reorganization.[14] Recent centralizations have almost all been the result of overwhelming economic pressures, the most decisive of which has been the need for construction of a new school. School boards may not be impressed with the annual financial and educational benefits derived from centralization, but the great cost of new school construction makes the central school construction grant too attractive to be ignored.[15]

CENTRALIZATION AND THE SUBURBS

Centralization has been as much a suburban as a rural process in upstate New York. Nevertheless, even with the advantage of concentrated populations, urban counties contain a good number of districts with fewer pupils in attendance than the already outdated 1,700 standard.

---

[14] New York has facilitated centralization by making it contingent upon approval of a majority of voters in the proposed district, rather than a majority within each participating district. But this move is still regarded as insufficient cause for reliance upon local initiative in effecting reorganization by Edward A. Bateman, *Development of the County-Unit School District in Utah* (New York: Bureau of Publications, Teacher's College, Columbia University, 1940), p. 93.

[15] A panel of New York educators judged that: "state aid for capital outlay . . . is the most important incentive for reorganization in New York. The influence of equalization aid and transportation allowances are somewhat controversial, although the weight of opinion seems to indicate that to some extent they are encouraging factors." Leslie L. Chisholm, *School District Reorganization* (Chicago: Midwest Administrative Centers, University of Chicago, 1957), p. 17. (This judgment was made prior to revisions in the transportation allowance that made it less advantageous for small districts to contract for the education of their pupils. Controversy over the equalization grant is still prevalent. Many still echo the sentiments of the Regents Inquiry, that equalization grants serve to maintain small and inefficient school units. *See* Grace and Moe, *op. cit.*, p. 214.

Table 4. Non-city School Districts Offering Kindergarten through 12th Grade, Fall, 1959

County	Area sq. miles	Pupil population (rounded)	No. of central districts	Sub-standard (less than 1700 pupils)	No. of union free districts	Sub-standard
Erie	1,054	74,000	17	2	6	
Monroe ...	673	39,000	12	2	3	1
Onondaga...	792	39,000	14	5	4	2
Oneida ...	1,227	32,000	13	8	3	3
Broome ...	910	20,000	9	3	3	
Albany	531	17,000	6	2	1	1
Rensselaer ..	665	13,000	7	5	1	
Niagara ...	533	13,000	6	1		
Herkimer ...	1,442	13,000	10	5	1	1
Schenectady	209	12,000	4	1	1	
Totals			98	34	23	8

SOURCE: State of New York Education Department, *Annual Report, 1959.*

Table 4 ranks the upstate urban counties by number of pupils attending non-city schools. It is not surprising to find that the four counties with the largest number of pupils also have the greatest number of school districts. But county area should also be considered in comparing numbers of districts. Historically, the need for large numbers of districts has been caused by the necessity to cover large territories. But the larger rural counties, with the aid of transportation, have been able to serve all their children with a fewer number of districts than smaller urban counties. Cattaraugus, Franklin, Hamilton, and Saint Lawrence Counties all have larger territories and fewer school districts than the urban counties.

If urban counties would enlarge their school districts to cover the same amount of territory as rural districts, they would in almost every instance exceed the state's attendance standards. But they seem deliberately not to have done so. Suburban districts are almost universally smaller than rural districts.

The tendency for suburban districts to be small in area is even more strikingly illustrated in the downstate suburban counties. In fact, the central school district is relatively a rarity in Nassau, Westchester, and Suffolk Counties. These three counties have enough population to support more than 130 union free districts which, for the most part, meet the state's pupil population standards. Because the downstate suburban districts have enough pupils, the state has not sought to press centralization upon them. As long as the centralization movement is dominated by the desire to meet a minimum population standard, there is little motivation to enlarge the territorial coverage of the downstate union free districts and the smaller central schools upstate.

But even if all suburban districts were to meet attendance standards, their proliferation would continue to present additional instructional and financial problems. Even districts of five and six thousand pupils find it impossible to construct and maintain technical or vocational high schools. Unless a child resides in a large city, he is usually unable to deviate from the standard, academic high-school curricula, whatever his capacity, aptitude, or inclinations. What opportunities do exist for specialized training are based upon short-term, renegotiable, often short-lived contracts.

The Nassau, Westchester, and Suffolk systems would collapse were it not for contracts. They contain more than sixty union free and central districts offering only grade-school courses. Some of these have as many as 4,000 pupils. Nassau's three central high school districts accommodate most of its elementary school districts. But there are more than 35,000 pupils in Suffolk County for whom the availability of a high-school education is dependent upon contracts with districts in which they do not reside.

Prior to 1956, contracting was financially advantageous to both sending and recipient districts. The Heald Commission initiated several formula changes to reduce financial benefits granted contracting districts and thus to stimulate more centralization. Today, sending districts often find it more economical to build a school than to transport children to outside districts, but contracts are still advantageous to many recipient districts. Contracting for students increases their average daily attendance, a major factor in the computation of state aid, without greatly increasing instructional costs or the required contribution to the foundation program. A brisk competition for contracting students still exists. It results in illogical and excessively costly transportation patterns and in the shifting of pupils from one high school to another, as contracts are renegotiated.

As continued population growth begins to tax existing facilities, contracting for outside students becomes less desirable for recipient districts. Sending districts have less choice in negotiation of contracts. Eventually the need for classrooms is so widespread that the sending district has no choice but to build its own school. This pattern is now emerging on Long Island. State officials expect educational localism on Long Island to give way to centralization, as the pressure for new construction increases the attractiveness of the broader tax bases and the additional state aid available for central school construction.

But if the participation of the centralized, upstate suburban counties in the "taxpayers' revolt" is indicative, centralization on Long Island may not appreciably reduce the burdensome cost of education. Centralization has offered temporary economic relief, but it has failed to resolve the two basic problems of educational organization:

1. Creation of districts large enough to maintain a complete range of educational facilities and offerings
2. Provision of a suitable tax base for the support of education and integrating this use of resources with other important demands for governmental expenditures.

These problems of instructional adequacy and financial capacity can be and have been treated independently of one another. The early centralization movement sought to increase the size of administrative units while shifting part of their financial burden to the state. However, the state's commitment to retain local initiative and responsibility precludes its complete assumption of program costs. As long as local districts continue to share in financing education, instructional, and financial objectives must be considered jointly in determining district size. But, with the exception of the enlarged, city school district, state policy is moving in the direction of treating organization for instructional purposes and organization for financial purposes independently.

The enlarged, city school district is not so much an attempt to broaden tax bases as it is to accommodate communities bordering on city boundaries. Significantly, it has not been used by any of the state's larger, independent, city school districts. It is, of course, limited to cities of less than 125,000 population. It would be politically and legally impractical to include non-city territory in a school district controlled by a legislature and executive elected only by city residents. Where it has been employed, the device has enabled fringe communities and cities to increase both instructional and financial capacities. The state has provided special aid to enlarged city districts to offset their ineligibility for transportation aid, but this aid is more a reimbursement for additional expenses than an incentive for enlargement.

The enlarged, city school district is not typical of recent

trends in state educational policy. Generally the state continues to follow a pattern of urban-rural separation. And it continues to experiment with special devices that tend to distinguish school finance from instructional service. One such device, the intermediate district, may be considered a second exception.

Intermediate districts were authorized in New York in 1948. They were designed as a means of gathering sufficient non-city population together to afford the maintenance of special instructional facilities. Although the intermediate district and its elected school board could operate its own schools, it was not intended to displace existing local districts. But the independent authority given the intermediate district was regarded as a threat to their own independence by the districts to be included in the intermediate unit and so discouraged any use of this new form of organization. Instead, school districts have been quick to join in the creation of Boards of Cooperative Educational Services.

The Board of Cooperative Educational Services was originally designed to serve as a transition to the intermediate district.[16] In its provision of special services to constituent districts, the board is similar to an intermediate unit, but it has no authority to own or purchase land or equipment. Unlike an intermediate district, it cannot operate schools but, instead, acts mainly as a contracting agent for participating school districts. The success of most of the eighty-three boards in arranging for the training of retarded children is indicative of the type of special service for which this unit is best adapted.

State aid, in limited amounts, is available to both the board and the intermediate district. But whereas the intermediate district is authorized, with the approval of constituent districts, to raise taxes to support its programs, the board is dependent upon contributions from its constituent districts for its finances.

[16] Memorandum of the State Education Department, *New York State Legislative Annual: 1955,* p. 166.

The distinction is critical and does much to explain the widespread use of the Board of Cooperative Educational Services and the reluctance to make the hoped-for transition to intermediate districts.

The federated district, the latest proposal by the State Education Department and the Governor, is a variation of the intermediate-district plan, shorn of any threats to the security of existing districts. The federated-district proposal is still in the formative stage in Albany, but the State Department of Education has already described it as particularly adaptable to metropolitan areas.[17]

The federated district would be formed for taxing purposes only. It would embrace all the school districts in one or a combination of counties. The proposal has not been developed to the point where the question of whether or not it will include fiscally dependent city districts must be answered. Component school districts would continue to raise their own taxes and operate their own schools. The federated district would provide them with additional revenues derived from sources that the individual districts are not now able to reach. The desire to use non-property taxes for school support is the real motivation for the proposal.

Except for the utilities tax which independent city districts are now authorized to levy and collect for themselves, all current applications of non-property taxes to school purposes are based on municipal largesse. These taxes are imposed and continued at the pleasure of county or city legislative bodies. In a sense, school districts are becoming fiscally dependent again.

Faced with the possibility of reversing the hard-won trend to fiscal independence, the Regents Inquiry chose to continue to

[17] The only available description of the proposal is the Governor's special message to the Legislature, reproduced in *The New York Times,* February 14, 1960, p. 60.

rely upon real estate for educational finances. The Heald Commission put the question to the legislature: "How [can we] provide local non-property taxing powers for fiscally independent and responsible school districts which will not involve fiscal dependence upon another unit of government."[18] The commission described in basic form what has come to be the concept of the federated school district. But implementation of this proposal involves problems of intergovernmental relations that go to the heart of the "metropolitan problem."

Many cities and several counties now collect non-real estate taxes for general revenue purposes. Are they to give up these sources of revenue to a competing governmental unit? If the federated district is authorized to levy sales or other taxes and distribute their proceeds to component districts, should it not have some measure of control over expenditures? As presently developed, the proposal calls for distribution to component districts on a population basis. This is the method by which Erie County distributes its sales tax receipts for the support of school districts. The City of Buffalo would probably object to any other formula. But the federated-district proposal is apt to be revised to incorporate an equalization principle. In any event, by separating the raising from the spending of money, the federated-district proposal represents virtual rejection of the promise of administrative unity held out by the intermediate district.

CONCLUSION

Separation is the keynote of state education policy. Except for the creation of enlarged, city school districts, state policy continues to treat the organization of city and rural or suburban school facilities differently despite the fact that cities and their surroundings are increasingly becoming less

[18] Temporary Commission on Educational Finances, *Financing Public Education in New York State, op. cit.*, p. 264.

distinguishable, demographically and economically. The fundamental principle of separation affecting education rests in its treatment as a preferred function, different from all others locally provided.

The Heald Commission found that it was impossible to determine the potential resources available for education in the "big six," apart from considering the potential needs of the general city governments. It suggested that these cities have greater difficulty in balancing educational and non-educational expenditures than smaller places, because of city residents' greater demands for governmental services. Are not the suburbs today faced with as great a need to balance services as cities?

By fostering the increased use of independent means of financing education, the state may be helping to resolve the immediate financial problems of local school districts, but it is scarcely contributing to metropolitan integration. In fact, by proposing to add yet another layer of school government to the multiplicity of governments in metropolitan areas, it appears to be doing quite the opposite.

The federated district plan promises further to fractionalize the distribution of services within metropolitan areas and to increase competition among independent governmental units. Commissioner Allen appears to be trying to blend the federated-district and intermediate-district proposals.[19] The failure of the intermediate-district proposal to date, however, offers little political hope for this eventuality. Even if it were to be accomplished, as long as education and other governmental functions are organized independently, competition will continue to exemplify their relationships.

Although it has had general success in reducing the number

---

[19] Despite the Governor's assurance that the federated district would be used only for taxing purposes, Allen continues to refer to it as a service unit for school construction, transportation, and special services.

of school districts, the centralization movement has had little metropolitan impact. It has not taken advantage of concentrated suburban populations to press for consolidations that would provide the specialized educational services available in central cities. The centralization movement has been inspired by the desire to create administrative units of sufficient pupil size to maintain an offering of general education courses. This limited goal today appears incapable of meeting modern requirements of specialized education and of integrating education with other local government activities.

It has been necessary to supplement centralization with several alternative cooperative devices in order to provide special services in the still too small central districts. These devices further complicate the educational system as well as the totality of governments in metropolitan areas.

Within the context of its limited goals, centralization has been achieved primarily as the result of economic pressures. Grant inducements have not in themselves stimulated centralization. Many communities have successfully resisted the enticement of state funds until the time when new construction became necessary. Economic necessity coupled with central-school construction aid has then become decisive.

It is not likely that grant incentives will be used to encourage adoption of the newer forms of organization now under consideration. The financial gains anticipated from the enlargement of tax bases and the pressures of mounting educational costs will probably be encouragement enough. The legislature appears to be content to authorize new forms of organization and new sources of revenue, leaving the determination to use them to local discretion.[20]

---

[20] The retention of local control is not the only motivation for the legislature's policy of leaving the imposition of new taxes to local authorities. The same educational supporters who raise the issue of home rule to defend the freedom of their school boards are now criticizing the

The state's apparent unwillingness to challenge local sentiment in regard to reorganization reflects the peculiar philosophy of authority that has developed as a result of educational separatism. Today, when some are pointing to education as the only true example of a function conducted in a metropolitan manner (that is without regard to city, town, and village boundaries), it is wise to examine the manner in which this metropolitan activity has been integrated with other area services.

Plainly, education has not been integrated. Educational leaders have been able to parlay their "uniqueness" into a position from which they will suffer no interference from other local governmental units or from the state itself. Education is a state function and as such is separate from local government. But educational pressure groups have succeeded in creating the impression that the Commissioner of Education is an outsider trying to coerce democratically elected school boards into action against their will.

Legally there is no home rule in education; but there certainly is independence, perhaps too much. The respect in which local independence is held by the state is well illustrated by a comment by Luther Gulick in 1938. He defended the Central Rural School District Act, noting that:

> [the Central Rural School District Act] continues in operation all of the schools brought together in the centralized district until the voters of the original district vote to close the school. This is a further guarantee that no "little red schoolhouse" will be abolished . . . until those who live around the school vote to close the school. . . .[21]

Save the little red schoolhouse!

---

legislature for failing to raise more money and for passing the onerous task of levying new taxes to local boards.

[21] Gulick, *op. cit.,* p. 92.

VI

Highways

THE SIGNIFICANT ROLE that transportation has played in the physical development of metropolitan areas is too well documented to require further comment here. Transportation is universally included among the first subjects for metropolitan research. Much of this research effort has been historical, documenting an observation that can generally be gained from visual impression; "highways were built and they determined land use."

Planning tools and techniques now available offer the opportunity of locating transportation facilities in accordance with a predetermined allocation of desirable land uses. As with most governmental activities, however, the utilization of planning skill is dependent upon the creation of a political framework and organizational structure in which technique can be democratically employed to effectuate community desire. In a metropolitan context, the political and organizational impact upon traffic-movement control is particularly important.

Although transportation refers to a number of means of movement, this study is limited to consideration of vehicular movement over highways, roads, and streets. Except for the unique New York Metropolitan Region, it is generally conceded that mass transportation is not publicly acceptable as a solution to the traffic and commuter problems of the nation. The use of private automobiles for daily commutation has become a cultural pattern, necessitating increased governmental commitment to highway building programs.[1] An Office of Transportation has recently been added to the Governor's Executive Office. Its mandate, in part, is to develop "policies and proposals designed to solve the special problems of urban and commuter transportation in metropolitan areas," involving both private- and mass-transportation facilities.[2] This office has yet, however, to provide leadership in planning for any means of transportation. For the foreseeable future, the metropolitan transportation problem will probably continue to be defined in terms of traffic movement, and its solution will probably rest with existing forms of governmental action.

Highways serve two metropolitan purposes: intermetropolitan and intrametropolitan movement. The former has long been an object of state and national concern, but intrametropolitan traffic has only recently been included as a major feature of national and state highway programs. Financing and planning highway construction in rural and urban areas has become increasingly the responsibility of state and national governments. Any discussion of highway development in metropolitan areas must then take into account the increasingly significant role of the federal and state governments in highway construction.

---

[1] Many continue to hope that mass-transportation facilities can be made more attractive, but realistically they concede that the private automobile will probably continue to increase in desirability as a daily means of transportation. Even in New York, Austin Tobin suggests, it is unrealistic to attempt to insist on mass transportation as an alternative for the private automobile, although Tobin is hardly a disinterested or objective observer. *See* Austin J. Tobin, "Transportation in the New York Metropolitan Region During the Next Twenty-Five Years," an address at the 25th Anniversary Regional Plan Conference, New York, Regional Plan Association, October 6, 1954, p. 28.

[2] New York, *Laws of 1959,* C. 16.

INTERGOVERNMENTAL HIGHWAY RELATIONS

Until the beginning of the twentieth century, roads were primarily a matter of local concern throughout the United States. Although most states had begun limited participation in highway administration prior to its passage, the Federal Highway Act of 1916 is generally credited with spurring state highway activities. Because the federal program was and still is centered on state administration, the scope of state highway activity has continually broadened since its inception.

The 1916 act established a classification of roads and a formula for allotment of federal grants that is still in use. States were allotted funds to develop primary and secondary systems of highways.[3] The dual designation represented a compromise between urban and rural interests. For the most part, the primary system served to connect urban and other traffic generating areas, while the secondary system was designed for "farm-to-market" use. However, both systems ended at city lines. Cities or more populous villages did not qualify for inclusion in either system.

The federal-grant program operates through a pattern of federal-state administrative relationships that differs significantly from the working relationships of state highway agencies and local officials. While local officials often regard the state's role as one of intervention, the federal Bureau of Public Roads has generally succeeded in imposing federal standards on state highway departments with a minimum of conflict and resentment. During the early years, the bureau provided the young and frequently ill-staffed state highway departments with sorely needed technical services. State officials met federal design and construction standards with little difficulty, and

[3] Actually, at this time, secondary roads were an adjunct of the primary system. States were allowed to devote a portion of the federal grant to secondary roads but were not required to do so. It was not until 1944 that a specific appropriation was provided for secondary highways.

early and continued technical consultation between state and federal officials resulted in a minimum of open friction.[4] Undoubtedly, the program's rural emphasis helped to minimize conflict, since federal requirements were less apt to evoke state objections when applied to the relatively cheap costs of rural land, as opposed to the higher costs and more complex problems of public relations in urban areas.

The patterns of federal-state relationships that emerged from the early years still prevail. The Bureau of Public Roads is consulted early and frequently in the planning of new or improved highways in the federal system. Once approved, construction is the sole responsibility of the state. Questions of how the work is to be done, maintenance, and financial arrangements between states and subsidiary local units are left to state determination. The states have thus been free to develop varying forms of highway administration. For the most part, the federal program has served to increase the professionalism of state highway agencies, to strengthen their position in regard to other state agencies and local officials, and to stimulate expanded state activity in highway affairs.

In New York, the federal program augmented a trend toward increased state participation in highway construction and finance that had begun at the turn of the century. The state had already designated a system of state highways that was to be its responsibility, as distinguished from the more local highways and roads in which it had lesser interest. These were incorporated into the federal system after 1916. Assumption of responsibility for state highways and the added responsibilities imposed by federal law led to progressive expan-

[4] In fact, "in some states the federal engineers are frequently consulted for advice on projects built entirely with state funds." V. O. Key, Jr., *The Administration of Federal Grants to States* (Chicago: Public Administration Service, 1937), p. 35.

sion of the state's role in highway development and to increased supervisory relations with local highway officials.

In accordance with federal policy, no federal funds were used for urban facilities. In fact, the state took no part at all in the highway affairs of cities or large villages. Even after 1933, when the federal law was amended to enable inclusion of urban facilities in the federal program, New York continued to limit its activities and financial support to rural areas.[5]

In 1944, urban arterials were designated as a third classification of highways eligible for federal aid. The urban arterial program was a belated recognition of the fact that the primary system had succeeded in funneling vehicles and people into narrow, congested, slow-moving city streets, where they were left to inch their way to city destinations or to state highways waiting at the other side of the city.

But conditions at the other side of the city were often no better than inside. The 1944 act authorized yet another federal system, the Interstate Highway System, subsequently renamed Interstate Defense Highway. It was designed to connect the principal metropolitan areas of the country. It provided for intraregional as well as interregional construction and, coupled with the urban arterial program, constituted the first national commitment to a program of highway construction to and *through* the nation's congested metropolitan areas. As presently planned, the Interstate system will link together 90 per cent of the cities having more than 50,000 population and will carry an estimated 20 per cent of the nation's traffic.[6]

The new federal program and the obviousness of postwar

---

[5] The amendment was enacted as part of the federal government's program to stimulate employment and was permissive only. Norman Hebden and Wilbur S. Smith, *State-City Relationships in Highway Affairs* (New Haven: Yale University Press, 1950), p. 99.

[6] The President's Advisory Committee on a National Highway Program, *A Ten Year National Highway Program: A Report to the President* (Washington, D.C., Government Printing Office, January, 1955), p. 7.

reconstruction needs led to the inclusion of urban arterials as part of New York's state highway system. For some time very little progress was made under the 1944 act. The Federal Aid Highway Act of 1956 was the first to provide sufficient funds to begin the huge program envisioned in 1944. The 1956 act provided for distribution of the increased funds in the following manner: 45 per cent primary; 30 per cent secondary; and 25 per cent urban arterial. A thirteen-year, 25 billion dollar program of interstate construction was authorized. The scope of the federal program as originally envisioned is indicated in the following table:

Table 5

Authorizations for Federal Highway Systems, 1957–1969
(in millions of dollars)

Year	Interstate $	Primary* $	Secondary* $	Urban Art* $	Total $
1957	1,175	371.25	247.5	206.25	2,000
1958	1,700	382.5	255.0	212.5	2,550
1959	2,200	393.75	262.5	218.75	3,075
1960	2,500	405.0	270.0	225.0	3,400
1961	2,000	416.25	277.5	231.25	2,925
1962	2,200				
1963	2,200				
1964	2,200				
1965	2,200				
1966	2,200				
1967	2,200				
1968	1,500				
1969	1,025				

* Authorizations for the primary, secondary, and urban arterial networks are made only on a two-year basis.

SOURCE: *United States Code Annotated,* Title 23, paras. 151 and 158.

It is difficult to determine the amounts New York is to receive from federal grants. Beginning with the fiscal year 1960, interstate funds are to be allotted to each state in the proportion that construction remaining to be done on its interstate highways bears to the total remaining construction on the system. Yearly appropriations and the total cost of the system will far surpass the original 25 billion dollar authorization.

Some indication of the federal program's impact on New York State can be gained from expenditure data recently released. In fiscal 1960, New York contracted for 303.7 million dollars of new highway construction, of which the federal government supplied 180.2 million and the state 123.5 million. Contracts to be awarded in fiscal 1961 are expected to require an expenditure of 292 million dollars, of which the federal government will supply 142 million and the state 150 million.[7]

Prior to the 1956 increase in federal appropriations, New York State had spent 189.7 million dollars for construction in fiscal 1956, of which 49.5 million was reimbursed by the federal government. In the same year, upstate local governments had spent 266.5 million dollars, most of which had been applied to maintenance and repairs.[8] Although more recent local expenditures are not available, it has been estimated that through 1960 they remained at the same level. Assuming they did, comparative expenditures for the years 1956, 1960, and 1961 would appear as in Table 6.

The picture that develops is one of increasing state and federal participation in the financing of new construction. While the availability of federal funds appears to have stabilized and reduced the proportion of state to local and federal expenditures respectively, this is no reflection on the importance of the state as a participa ıt in highway construction, for

---

[7] *New York Times,* April 8, 1960, p. 1.

[8] State of New York, Temporary Highway Finance Planning Commission, *Fifth Report,* Legislative Document No. 58 (1958) pp. 7–9.

federal funds are paid to and managed by the state government.

Table 6. Comparative Expenditures for Highway Construction, New York State
(in millions of dollars)

	New Construction		Maintenance and Construction
	State	Federal	Upstate local
	$	$	$
1956 (actual)	140.2	49.5	266.5
1960 (local estimated)	123.5	180.2	270.
1961 (estimated)	150.0	142.0	270.

Although we are accustomed to refer to the impact of federal programs upon metropolitan areas, the federal highway program's impact is, in reality, felt as administered by the state government. To be sure, design standards and general route location are a function of the Bureau of Public Roads, But the more immediate impact of route designation and construction priorities is a product of the detailed planning and construction activities of the New York State Department of Public Works. This highly professional state agency enjoys generally satisfactory relationships with the federal agency and is granted a great deal of discretion within the broad limits of federal requirements. Since the end of the Second World War, the responsibility for major highway construction throughout the state has continually shifted to the state and its Department of Public Works.

Although the need for new highway construction is the most dramatic aspect of the metropolitan traffic problem, it is only one factor affecting the current and future problem of moving vehicles and people. The streets, roads, and feeder highways that serve the major routes, and the terminal facilities that accommodate the increased interregional movement made possible by the state and federal construction programs, are equally pressing problems to metropolitan residents. Their state of repair, maintenance, and traffic control all contribute to the overall adequacy of traffic facilities.

The federal and state governments have virtually ignored parking, in their concern for vehicular movement. The urban arterial program is particularly affected by this intentional oversight. For years, political leaders have been besieged with conflicting demands by traffic engineers and commercial and other interests. The use of streets for traffic movement or for parking is a politically loaded issue. The urban arterial program represents a clear victory for traffic movement, but it has not been accompanied by any effort to provide terminal facilities. No federal or state funds are available for parking facilities or, perhaps even more important, for the integration of existing city thoroughfares with the new arterials.

Integration of town, village, and county thoroughfares is only slightly better provided. For the most part, the federal and state programs have been superimposed upon the preexisting, fragmented system of highway administration, with its complex of intergovernmental relationships.

THE HIGHWAY SYSTEM

New York's highway network is composed of five systems: state highways, county roads, town highways, municipal streets (city and village), and highway and bridge facilities operated by special authorities. The highway law covers only the state, county, and town systems. Municipal streets are generally outside the state's jurisdiction. Although the special authorities significantly affect movement within the state, with the exception of the State Thruway, they are most important as revenue devices to finance short-route needs.

Mileage for which the state is exclusively responsible consists of 13,000 miles of highways and urban arterials. Almost all of this mileage is part of the federal system in one form or another. Most of the 19,000 miles of county roads are on the federal secondary system. There are more than 42,000 miles of improved town roads and approximately 13,000 more miles unimproved.

Table 7. Highway Mileage in New York State, 1957

	State	County	Town	Special	Municipal	Total
Fed. aid, primary...	9,038	361		777	368	10,544
Fed. aid, secondary	4,001	14,547		7		18,555
Non-fed. aid	176	4,068	55,467	367	16,377	76,457
Total	13,217	18,976	55,467	1,151	16,745	105,556

SOURCE: United States Department of Commerce, *Highway Statistics, 1957.*

The construction and maintenance of the three components of the state system are integrated through a complex system of mapping and supervision, which stems from federal requirements. In recent years, there has been comparatively little new location of highways. Instead, the progressive increases in state and county mileages have been due to the reconstruction of existing road beds, so that they meet federal standards for inclusion in the federal-aided categories. Once accepted as a primary or secondary highway, the new mileage is included in the computation of federal aid but is maintained and improved by the governmental unit having jurisdiction over it.

The designation of county roads as federal-aid secondary highways does not lead to any direct federal-county relationships. New York is one of many states that have entered into agreement with the Bureau of Public Roads to assume responsibility for guaranteeing adherence to federal standards on the secondary system. But this guarantee does not result in increased state control of county roads on the secondary system. These roads are a local responsibility, subject to the same state supervision exercised over all local highways. Only a small portion of county roads are actually built with federal funds. When so built, the road is taken over by the state for the period of construction and then returned to the county for maintenance and control.

State Highways. All designations of the routes and locations of state highways are legislatively determined upon the recommendation of the State Department of Public Works. The official state highway map, originally begun in 1908, shows all existing routes and those planned for inclusion in the state system, either through new construction or through the improvement of local thoroughfares up to state standards.

Construction, planning, and location of state highways is the sole responsibility of the Department of Public Works. The cost is borne entirely by the state, except for additional costs incurred for special features requested by localities. One interesting limitation of the state's program is the requirement that the department receive approval from county Boards of Supervisors prior to relocating or limiting access on an existing state route. While this limitation might appear to lessen state freedom of action, it does not apply to state highways primarily designed for through-traffic movement. Most state facilities qualify for this exclusion.

Maintenance, improvement, and traffic control on state highways are the responsibility of the Department of Public Works. In the past, counties shared in the cost of maintenance and snow removal. Today, most counties continue to service state highways under contract with the department, but receive total reimbursement for their efforts.

County Roads. Planning, construction, maintenance, and

traffic control on county roads is the responsibility of the County Engineer or Highway Superintendent, working under the direction of the Board of Supervisors. The county highway official also exercises supervision over the activities of town highway superintendents.

County construction activities are not limited to the county road system alone. Counties are authorized to help construct or improve town highways upon request. The costs of such projects may be financed as a general county charge or as a town charge. Because the costs of joint projects are included as county expenditures, they are included in the computation of state aid to counties. Thus state aid paid to counties is listed as aid to counties and towns, and it is difficult to determine what portion is being applied to county roads or to town highways.

Town Highways. Town highways are under the immediate supervision of town highway superintendents. These officials are almost all elected. State aid for town highways is annually available on an equalization basis. In addition, in 1950, a special ten-year grant program for town highway improvement was authorized. This so-called Erwin Plan aid is available to 1962. To date its results have not been outstanding, although it has been responsible for the improvement of several thousand miles of town highways.[9]

Urban Arterials. Urban arterials are extensions of federally aided state highways into cities. Their construction follows the general procedures of federal-state participation, except for some modifications imposed by the state legislature in regard to arterials on the primary and secondary systems. In 1944, the legislature authorized construction of 579 miles of arterials. Although the arterials were to be part of the state highway

[9] *See* State of New York, Department of Public Works, *Annual Report, 1959,* p. 71.

system, cities were required to share equally in the costs of obtaining rights-of-way.

It has been suggested that cost sharing was motivated as much by political and administrative as by financial reasons. Cost sharing was in part designed

> . . . to foster a locally realistic view as to the scale of any proposals for arterial routes. At the same time this would give the cities a control over the scope and details of the plan as conceived by the state—for without local appropriation, projects considered undesirable by a city could not be advanced.[10]

It is apparent that cities regard this control as a dubious advantage. It is essentially negative, for in practice the cities' participation in planning consists merely of the ability to veto plans submitted by the state. Since 1956, wherever possible, the state has shifted urban arterials to the interstate system, where they qualify for 90 per cent reimbursement, as opposed to 50 per cent on the primary and secondary federal-aid systems. Cities are not required to contribute to interstate arterials. None has objected to the transfer.[11]

STATE-LOCAL HIGHWAY RELATIONS

Three forms of state-local contact affect the metropolitan transportation problem. First, and increasingly becoming more important, are the construction activities of the state itself. Financial contributions to local highway activities and the resulting supervisory controls delegated to the Superintendent of Public Works are a second point of contact. A third and most basic form derives from the state's general authority to prescribe the form and duties of local governments.

---

[10] Hebden and Smith, *op. cit.*, p. 108.

[11] Binghamton continues to be most vocally opposed to having to share in acquisition costs for arterials not on the interstate system. *See* its Mayor's testimony at "Public Hearing of the New York State Joint Legislative Committee on Metropolitan Area Study at Binghamton, New York, on December 10, 1958" (mimeographed), pp. 16–18.

Form and Duties. Except for recommendations stemming from the generally critical studies of local government in the late 1920's and early 1930's, there has been little serious consideration of revising the traditional road responsibilities of New York's local governments. New York is one of thirteen states maintaining a tripartite division of rural highway activities between state, county, and town governments. Although no state has yet assumed more than a minimal responsibility for urban facilities, four have undertaken state administration of all rural roads, a number have eliminated the town or its equivalent as a unit of administration, and Connecticut has recently eliminated the county.[12]

Several variations of the traditional organization have occurred in New York. The most significant is the cooperative system of road maintenance and improvement developed in Monroe County. Through contracts with town highway departments, the county has virtually been able to give up its own work forces. Instead, it utilizes town crews for work on county roads and through a central dispatching office is able to transfer crews from one location to another depending upon where their efforts are most needed. While this system provides for a more unified approach to maintenance needs throughout the county and for more effective utilization of manpower, it does not affect the towns' basic responsibility for their own systems.

With more than 80,000 miles of rural highways to be serviced, some degree of decentralization is unavoidable. But proponents of the elimination of towns as units of highway administration contrast the need for decentralization of maintenance with the need for centralization and integration of

[12] Paul W. Wager, *County Government Across the Nation* (Chapel Hill: University of North Carolina Press, 1950), pp. 27–28; and United States Department of Commerce, *Highway Statistics, 1957.*

new planning and construction. They do not object to towns maintaining work forces, but do criticize the presently inadequate coordination of multijurisdictional highway activities.

A recent attempt to consolidate highway activities in Illinois offers an interesting parallel to the plans harbored by some New York officials for utilizing grants-in-aid as a centralizing device. An administration bill introduced in the Illinois legislature called for withholding grants to towns and road districts maintaining only a few miles of roads. In time, the bill would have resulted in the reduction of approximately one-third the number of units engaging in highway construction. However, even after successive legislative amendments had reduced the mileage requirement to where it was no longer very effective, the proposal failed to gain approval.[13]

New York has never attempted to mandate consolidation of highway units, nor has it ever gone so far as to authorize consolidation. To the contrary, the state now appears to be encouraging continued decentralization. At a time when other states were questioning the adequacy of continued reliance on local units, New York enacted the Erwin Plan, committing itself to the further bolstering of town highway units rather than their replacement. The political forces motivating this act are fairly obvious. In view of the increasing number of functions being transferred to counties, highway management looms as the major activity politically and administratively justifying the retention of town government. The political consequences of reorganising highway activities are so great as to make it highly improbable that towns will be relieved of highway responsibilities in the near future.

Supervisory Relations. Short of reorganizing the structure of highway units, integration of policy and administration may

---

[13] State of Illinois, *Local Road Administrative Units,* Illinois Legislative Council, Publication 127, November, 1956, p. 33.

be achieved through the actions of state officials as coordinators of local activities. Indeed, a review of the Superintendent of Public Works' legal authority to prescribe design standards and the many approvals required from him before local authorities can act leaves the impression that the state is a most important participant in local policy determination.

State supervision of local highway activities has largely been a product of both the federal and state grant-in-aid systems. The absence of state supervision of city and village programs is directly related to their exclusion from grant eligibility. Although state reports often fail to make the distinction, state contributions to local highway finance consist of two forms of payment : shared taxes and grants-in-aid.

The state shares receipts from motor vehicle registrations and fuel taxes with counties. After previously having been denied a share in these sources, New York City was included in the sharing of registration receipts in 1958. Grants to counties and towns are awarded on a matching and equalization basis respectively. State payments to counties match county contributions to the road fund but are limited to not more than $30 per mile of county roads. Town aid represents the difference between the proceeds of a town tax of one-half mile per dollar of real property valuation and the sum of $150 per mile of town highways, in no case being less than $75 per mile. Needless to say, state aid as distinguished from shared taxes represents only a small portion of local expenditures for highway improvement and repairs.

The 1958 record of payments bears quantitative witness to the *quid pro quo* tactics that dominate upstate-downstate legislative relations. The 10 million dollar increase in shared taxes resulted primarily from the inclusion of New York City in the distribution and partially from continued increase in the number of vehicles registered. It was accompanied, however, by an unusually large increase in other payments to upstate units.

Table 8. State Payments to Local Governments for Highway Purposes, 1950–1958

(in millions of dollars)

Year	Shared taxes $	County and town aid $	Town aid $	Erwin Plan $
1950	20,430	2,012	2,922	
1951	21,179	2,049	2,911	
1952	21,935	2,111	2,909	
1953	25,989	2,124	2,916	3,534
1954	26,206	2,860	2,208	4,139
1955	28,837	2,837	2,209	4,652
1956	29,894	2,161	2,934	4,828
1957	32,138	2,900	2,209	4,954
1958	42,607	3,726	4,703	6,355

SOURCE: State of New York, *Comptrollers Report: 1956, 1957, 1958* (p. 173, 67, 68).

Table 8 does not include state reimbursements for snow removal and other services provided on state highways by local units, nor does it take into account direct state and federal expenditures on the federal secondary system. In itself, the table does indicate to some extent the level of state support of local highway activities. In 1956, counties and towns spent 140 million dollars on roads and highways, almost 40 million of which came from state sources.[14]

Although the greater portion of state payments is in the form of shared taxes rather than grants-in-aid, resulting in a justifiable inclination for recipients to regard the two differently, both serve to support the requirement of state approval of local procedures and expenditures. Furthermore, the Superintendent of Public Works' review authority extends past

[14] Temporary Highway Finance Planning Commission, *op. cit.*, p. 7.

expenditures to projected plans. The superintendent's authority to disapprove projects and withhold state payments is rarely invoked but is a dormant power that may be used to influence local action.

County superintendents are required to file a map of county roads with the department. Once approved, the map becomes the official basis for computing state aid. Each year, the county must file a work plan with the department indicating projects to be undertaken on the official map. Prior to any expenditure of county road funds (including both state and local moneys) the work plan must have been approved by the County Board of Supervisors and the Superintendent of Public Works. The board's approval is not required for plan modifications subsequently agreed to by the county and highway executives.

Even closer ties govern the relationships between county and town highway officials. County engineers perform most of the study and design work on town highways upon request of town superintendents. County highway officials have ultimate responsibility for supervising the award of town contracts and the acceptance of additions to the town system. Major town purchases of equipment and supplies require prior approval from county superintendents. A town work plan, similar to that filed by the county with the state, is the basis for town-county negotiations and agreements.

The highway coordination resulting from this interlocking supervisory arrangement is more apparent than real. Its effectiveness is lessened by a number of circumstances, prime among them being the system's basic orientation. The planning and supervisory arrangements are operationally oriented. They fail to attack the underlying problem of highway administration in metropolitan areas: the lack of coordinated planning for long-range traffic and development needs.

Indeed, there is little long-range planning being done on an individual basis. As the volume and costs of the mere maintenance of highways continue to mount, local units have been able to do little more than try to keep pace with the backlog of needed repairs on existing thoroughfares. Their work plans, far from projecting future needs, represent a piecemeal attempt to minimise the political consequences of the most serious of current local complaints. Under the circumstances, reviewing authorities hesitate to impose their judgments upon local political necessities. County officials are particularly sensitive to the elected status of Town Superintendents. Although the opportunity for intervention exists and working relationships vary, often depending upon the political allegiances of local officials, county engineers generally do not intercede in town highway affairs.

Consequently, the supervisory system has tended toward legalistic and technical review of contract specifications, award procedures, and expenditures. Its failure to produce comprehensive and coordinated planning was evident almost at its inception and was one of the reasons for the state's entrance into construction activities. Political, economic, and technical forces similar to those that led New York to assume partial control of rural highways are now propelling the state into urban highway activity. But, having experienced dissatisfaction with the grant-in-aid and supervisory system as tools for the development of rural networks, the state has centered its urban program exclusively upon state planning and construction.

State Highway Construction. In its earliest form, state concern for rural highways was the result of economic and political factors that still affect metropolitan highway development. The grant-in-aid system was the particular result of difficulties surrounding the applicability of the nineteenth-century labor system of constructing and maintaining roads to the twentieth-century motor age. By means of grants, the state attempted to shift local work methods from dependence upon extraction of labor from townspeople to the more dependable and technically satisfactory results obtainable from payment for services financed by state grants and local taxes.[15]

The labor system had proved inadequate in two respects. Local labor evidently lacked the skills necessary to meet modern highway needs. In addition, the labor system was financially unsuitable to many towns bordering large urban centers. Their political leaders asserted that city dwellers were deriving benefits from rural roads without physically or financially sharing in their construction. The monetary system was intended to remedy both these inadequacies.[16]

In regard to the economic motivation, it is interesting to note that today the distribution of shared taxes to counties only is defended on the grounds of the benefits provided cities by rural access roads. But with New York City having been made eligible for a share of motor vehicle registration receipts in 1958, it is to be expected that other municipalities will increase their demands for a share of these tax sources.

By 1898, the availability of state funds had stimulated the beginning of a joint state and county highway network. But within a few years, state officials grew dissatisfied with the results obtained from cooperation with and dependence upon county governments. The county and state highways were removed from county auspices and became the nucleus of the state highway system.

A similar pattern governed the development of the county

---

[15] State of New York, Special Joint Committee on Taxation and Retrenchment, *Report, 1926,* Legislative Document No. 68 (1926), pp. 23–24.

[16] W. M. Curtiss, *The Development of Highway Administration and Finance in New York* (Ithaca, New York: New York State College of Agriculture, Cornell University, 1936), p. 24.

road system. County roads were at first planned and built through the cooperation of town and county officials. Counties received grants from the state and apportioned funds among towns for the construction of county roads. The direction of the work was supervised by a committee of highway officials consisting of the county superintendent, three members of the board of supervisors, and the town supervisor of a town in which construction was occurring. The system was not very satisfactory, often becoming mired in the jealousies and disputes of town officials, and resulting in the completion of short lengths of highways with little coordination between them.[17]

To provide better coordination on the county system, counties were authorised to construct roads independently of towns in 1929. Roads were to be built under the direct supervision of the county superintendent and were to conform to projected maps of the county systems to be approved by the state superintendent of public works. Having in many cases invested heavily in equipment and personnel in anticipation of work on county roads, the towns tried unsuccessfully to block passage of the authorizing legislation. But their fears proved groundless, as the requirements of the towns' highway systems were more than enough to occupy their accumulated resources.

State highways activities have become progressively more removed from local participation. At first, local units were required to contribute to state maintenance and to snow removal. The Department of Public Works' later assumption of complete operating and financial responsibility for state highways, although primarily intended to reduce the drain on local resources, was also intended to secure more uniform road conditions on the state system. Although state highways continue to be serviced by local forces, the department has

[17] *Ibid.*, p. 41.

found that it can achieve better results through contracting with and reimbursing local units for services, while retaining the capacity to act in its own behalf, then through requiring local contributions.

Prior to the beginning of the urban arterial program, the state had already assumed independent responsibility for every stage of its highway program, planning, design, land acquisition, construction, and maintenance. The urban program granted two major concessions to municipal home rule: one the privilege of paying for one-half the cost of land acquisition, the other the authority to approve or disapprove state arterial plans. Arterials forming connections to the Interstate System required no financial participation by cities.

Although all urban arterials are so designated by state legislation, both city and state officials are authorized to draw plans for new routes. However, city planners rarely participate in the early stages of highway planning. In the program's first few years, city officials occasionally gained their first knowledge of a proposed arterial when presented with state plans submitted for their approval. Today, more amicable relationships have been worked out, but planners still complain of state arbitrariness, authoritarianism, and indifference to local demands.

Despite the difficulties of its program, the Department of Public Works remains the only agency capable of planning a coordinated highway network leading to and through metropolitan centers. And for all their complaints, city officials are in a position to do little else but accept the findings and plans of state engineers. The proposed arterials are too costly and too necessary for the relief of local traffic congestion to be delayed because of professional or political jealousies. An even greater stake centers around the arterial's place within the primary or interstate systems. Since most arterials are planned as urban extensions of primary or interstate routes, a delay in completion of the urban arterial, accompanied by completion of other sections of the route, may divert suburban traffic from the city and permanently affect patterns of commutation for social, cultural, or economic purposes. The competitive location of upstate metropolitan areas makes this last factor an important consideration affecting state-local relations in the approval of arterial plans.

The state's construction program has been criticized for its slowness and, according to municipal critics, for the secrecy in which the state conducts its planning. They assert that state officials are not only slow in developing plans but also non-communicative and secretive in not disclosing their contents until they are almost in the final stages. At issue is more than local resentment at not being informed or consulted. Urban-renewal officials and city planners maintain that their operations require intimate knowledge of plans for future highway construction and that, pending the disclosure of state plans, they must delay their own activities or chance the possibility of later program conflict.

Urban and rural political leaders also assail the state's secrecy or indecisiveness. They face the task of conditioning local response to land condemnations and highway construction. They attribute the attitude of state officials to indifference, borne of bureaucratic centralization and aloofness from local political sentiment. Indeed, the highly centralized nature of the state's operation, with almost all planning taking place in Albany, lends surface support to their allegations.

State engineers counter with arguments of their own. They refuse to bear full responsibility for the conflicts among highway construction, planning, and urban renewal. After all, coordination at the federal level has certainly not been achieved, and, even if they were free to plan their own arterial systems, there would be no guarantee that local officials could integrate highways with planning and redevelopment.

In reply to charges of secrecy, state officials point to the necessity for lengthy negotiations with federal officials prior to the completion of detailed plans. Local officials are not completely in the dark, they maintain, since the general plan for highway location is available in legislation. More detailed plans cannot be revealed prematurely for fear of encouraging real estate speculation in advance of actual construction and subsequent higher costs of condemnation.

Since the cost of interstate urban arterials is borne entirely by the state and federal governments, it has been possible in this program to initiate advance land acquisition long before the completion of final plans and designs. Where employed, advance acquisition has reduced the length of time required for condemnation and the beginning of construction, while also serving to notify local officials of state intentions.[18] But at the same time, advance acquisition represents a firmer psychological, as well as financial, commitment to preliminary state plans and makes it that much more difficult for localities to negotiate with state engineers for changes.

On the positive side, there is little doubt that the state, stimulated by the federal government, has brought to the problem of providing access to and through metropolitan areas financial and technical resources that would otherwise not have been available. The state has assisted localities in upgrading their own facilities, through the enforcement of standards and the insistence upon and often the provision of research services.

The state's greatest contribution, however, has been its own construction program. The traffic volume borne on state highways, their ability to traverse the state and each individual

[18] State of New York, Department of Public Works, *Annual Report: 1958,* p. 18.

county from end to end, and, currently, their capacity to link rural and suburban fringes directly to metropolitan centers testify to the state's significant accomplishments in metropolitan transportation. Although success has often been achieved at the price of ignoring or overriding local sensitivities and objections, bigger and better highways have been built.

CONCLUSION

In reviewing actions stimulated by metropolitan conditions, the Hughes Committee pointed to the huge scale of federal and state highway programs and activities, noting that they have resulted in the absence of local adaptations to highway needs similar to those undertaken with regard to other metropolitan problems.[19] The effectiveness of the state's highway program is, however, less readily attested to than its importance. A true evaluation, if intended to weigh state action as opposed to other possible forms of organization, must isolate those elements of the program that reflect the state's role per se.

Some observers of intergovernmental relations in New York State attribute the state's success in building new urban arterials to the objectivity that characterizes its highway planning and construction process. They conclude that

> the selection of the system is made on the basis of all the factual data that can be assembled—population growth and density, land-use data, assessed valuations, as well as origin and destination and other comprehensive traffic survey data. Once the arterial system is selected, a definite part of the planning procedure involves compiling a program of projects and determining both the order of construction and the estimated cost.
>
> These urban area studies are made by the state and upon completion are submitted to the city authorities for approval.

---

[19] State of New York, Joint Legislative Committee on Metropolitan Areas Study, *Metropolitan Action: A Six-County Inventory of Practical Programs, op. cit.* p. 37.

While there are some weaknesses, the procedure does provide a sound, planned approach to the whole problem. Further, it immediately fixes the state's responsibility, administratively and financially. The various pressures, local and otherwise, to be brought to bear on both the state and city officials are reduced to a minimum.[20]

Local officials would probably amend the above evaluation by characterizing the state's objectivity as a method, not of minimizing pressures, but of avoiding them. They would suggest that these pressures represent vital and valid public and official concern for problems that are perhaps more important than traffic movement: land use adjoining highways, property values, and future development of the city and its environs. They object to state engineers showing more concern for origin and destination studies and other data influencing the automotive choice of highways than for projecting the impact of highways on future community development.[21]

Local planners are particularly critical of the limited orientation of state engineers. They point out that state activities have a much greater impact than the mere relief of traffic congestion. The construction of state highways and the alterations of local streets and roads that they necessitate can materially change and influence the physical appearance, as well as the social and economic characteristics, of whole neighborhoods. Yet this program is directed, with a minimum of local participation, by an agency located in Albany that employs not a single city planner.

[20] Hebden and Smith, *op. cit.*, p. 182.

[21] Within cities, the latter consideration is particularly important. At least the President of Binghamton's City Council felt so when he testified at a Hughes Committee hearing, "The State in planning highways has apparently given no thought to the sociological or economic effect of these highways on the city." "Public Hearing of the New York State Joint Legislative Committee on Metropolitan Areas Study at Binghamton, N.Y., on December 10, 1958," p. 19.

At first glance, the dispute appears to be one that is as likely to occur intragovernmentally as intergovernmentally, a dispute arising from differences in the training, orientation, and objectives of engineers and planners. To be sure, this is one element contributing to the program's difficulties. But, the dispute is fundamentally based upon differences in policy orientation rather than professional training. In the final analysis, state and federal officials fall back on the convenient legal façade that theoretically justifies their interest in expanding highway programs—its interstate and defense nature. Although they cannot deny their program's metropolitan importance, they are concerned with both greater and lesser issues: construction of a national transportation network, and the completion of individual sections of roads.

Of more far-reaching importance, the dispute involves the feasibility of taking one metropolitan problem out of context and entrusting its solution to an agency removed from local political control; for with the state's assumption of responsibility for major traffic arteries in metropolitan areas, the treatment of highway problems apart from other metropolitan problems was virtually assured. In following any other course, state engineers would be obliged to sacrifice the one great advantage they now enjoy—objectivity.

By acceding to the planners' demands, state officials would necessarily become embroiled in local planning and politics. Indeed, they are now, but as effectors rather than participants. New York's Republican-dominated state legislature may well be able to afford to engage Robert Moses and the City of New York in open conflict over the criteria governing the location of and approaches to a Narrows Bridge. The State Department of Public Works cannot. New York State is in no position to engage in local planning. State engineers find their natural inclination to follow engineering rather than planning criteria, bolstered by their organizational goals of objectivity, speed, and economy. They retreat further into their own statistical world of origin and destination studies and traffic surveys—a world in which zoning, planning, and considerations of social consequences have no place.

In the years to come, the problems now associated with planning and building urban arterials will certainly spread to surrounding areas that have yet to reach their peak of population and land value. Already the city critics are being joined by voices from suburban and less urban areas where, with metropolitan sophistication, land use, planning, and zoning are becoming everyday terms.[22] "If the future highway needs of New York are to be met without continued friction, adaptations in present intergovernmental arrangements will undoubtedly have to be made. These may occur in either of two directions: by reinvesting local governments (or a new local unit) with complete responsibility for highways, as well as for planning, or by devising means of injecting new values and emphases into the state program.

To some extent, the latter course is now being followed, but with only slight success. Each of the county and/or Regional Planning Boards that now encompass most of the state's urban counties has brought into the local planning process the State Department of Public Works' District Engineer responsible for its territory, either as an advisory or ex officio member or as an invited participant. Unfortunately, in their busy schedules, District Engineers are not always able to attend board meetings. Furthermore, local officials fear that little of the rapport

[22] The most ardent spokesman for county planners was the late Hugh Pomeroy (although he represented a county much advanced in metropolitan sophistication). *See* his criticisms of the state program in his testimony at "Public Hearing of the New York State Joint Legislative Committee on Metropolitan Areas Study at the Westchester County Office Bldg. on June 10, 1958" (Mimeographed) pp. 18–36.

established at the infrequent meetings filters up to the highway planners and engineers in Albany.

A possibility of more effectively altering the state's values and perhaps also of rebalancing the influences of participants in metropolitan highway and planning decisions is suggested by 1962 amendments to the Federal-Aid Highway Act. They require that after July 1, 1965, the Secretary of Commerce

> shall not approve under section 105 of this title any program for projects in any urban area of more than fifty thousand population unless he finds that such projects are based on a continuing comprehensive transportation planning process carried on cooperatively by States and local communities in conformance with the objectives stated in this section.

What is a continuous comprehensive transportation planning process? And what will be the degree of state-local cooperation that will satisfy the objectives of the law? Its objectives are undoubtedly to minimize the friction between state highway construction and local planning, forcing both to be responsive to each other. But more than planning, as such, is involved. The law seeks to impress upon state highway officials responsibility for the impact of their decisions on metropolitan development. The comprehensiveness of transportation planning has been defined by the Secretary to include not only a geographic scope, but also consideration of

> social and community-value factors, such as, preservation of open space, parks and recreational facilities; preservation of historical sites and buildings; environmental amenities; and aesthetics.[23]

How is the state to take these factors into account? Several alternatives have been suggested. One is to develop regional transportation planning agencies in which state highway

---

[23] U.S. Department of Commerce, Bureau of Public Roads, *Instructional Memorandum50-2-63, 38–40,* March 27, 1963.

officials, and representatives from other state agencies, will participate along with members representing local governments. A second might be a more formal relationship with Regional Planning Boards, supported by written agreements as required by law. Yet a third might be the establishment of formal agreements between the state and each of the local units in urban areas.

Whatever formal arrangements are made to satisfy the law's requirements, they are certain to affect the state's ability to act quickly and the capacity for detachment that, in part, has led to the state's assumption of increasing responsibility for highway decisions in metropolitan areas. The Secretary has indicated that state highway departments will be expected to show that "scrupulous efforts" have been made to obtain *cooperative* transportation planning. The future will reveal what sacrifice of state interests will thus be entailed and how long and how well the inherent conflicts among localities and between them and the state can be accommodated through cooperation.

In contrast to the earlier rural program, the state's urban highway program has been beset with difficulties that can be expected to increase as urban social, political, and economic complexities spread with metropolitan expansion. Fitting a state construction program into the already complicated network of local programs in metropolitan areas is difficult in itself. The basically different approaches that state and local officials bring to the problem of highway construction compound the dilemma. Unless these differences can be resolved, local officials and impartial observers may still be saying in future years: the state is building highways, but it is creating more problems than it is solving.

VII

Tools of State Influence

THE FUNCTIONS discussed in the four chapters immediately preceding were selected for examination on two bases of representativeness. They illustrate, first, an array of metropolitan problems of varying degrees of urgency and popular recognition. Second, they operate through patterns of state-local relations that embrace the full range of techniques for influencing local action available to the state.

Consolidation of local health units represents a professional response to a metropolitan problem which as yet has failed to arouse the interest and concern of most citizens. Public health, as well as police, welfare, and a host of other local services constitute the bulk of what the professionals label the *metropolitan problem*. Support for their reorganization along metropolitan lines is founded upon administrative and professional objectives—economies of scale, increased services, policy and organizational coordination and integration—lacking sufficient public attractiveness to overcome local social, economic, political, and psychological commitments to decentralization and fragmentation. Suburban citizens are not dying for want of county health departments. They may well view formation of such agencies as a severe challenge to their present governmental system and the values it serves.

Partly due to the absence of dramatic public-health issues and partly in response to a related lack of effective demand political professionals have been slow in implementing the functional professionals' reorganization plans. Although political leaders occasionally consider mandating reorganization, the state's efforts are primarily directed at generating local support for change through public education, paving the way for the exercise of local initiative through permissive legislation and providing financial stimulants that will hopefully make county health departments attractive to local decision makers. The success of the state's activities has been partially negated, however, by the effectiveness of its own past efforts to increase the level of public-health services locally available.

In controlling water pollution, metropolitan areas face a problem more recognizable than public health organization and one that has more widespread appeal and more economically serious consequences. As a result, state policy has been more forceful in attempting to secure local compliance with state standards. Legislation permitting cooperative action has been accompanied by legislative and administrative encouragement of interlocal action. Moreover, although the pollution-control grant program is as yet too small to be of much influence, the Water Pollution Control Board's enforcement powers intimate a possible use of coercion that local leaders find hard to ignore.

Public education is not easily categorized as a metropolitan problem. To be sure, it is a matter of considerable public concern, but not in characteristically metropolitan terms. The lack of a metropolitan identification attaching to education is partly due to the traditional policy of separating education from other municipal functions. Financial perspective is especially affected by educational separation. Furthermore, the tradition has had the effect of denying the educational system the one possible advantage accruing to it from metropolitan growth, the concentration of pupil population in numbers sufficient to support diversified and specialized curricula. Here too, the values served by decentralization repeatedly triumph over professional urgings, even, or perhaps especially, when an activity considered so vital by many individuals is concerned.

Although public education is generally regarded as a state responsibility, New York's method of influencing local action is here judged to lie somewhere between the extremes of hopeful persuasion, sweetened with the enticement of preferential grants-in-aid, and legislative coercion. Mandate is as much out of the question in education as health, despite the obvious differences in the state's formal responsibility for the two functions.

The state's methods of dealing with education are similar to those employed in other programs. Educational policy, however, illustrates the fullest development of the functional approach to metropolitan problems, and educational organization exemplifies the ultimate refinement of the single-purpose, special district, metropolitan solution.

A sense of urgency has for so long dominated discussions of the metropolitan transportation problem, that few citizens can have escaped its impact. Transportation constitutes the major physical problem of metropolitan areas at the same time that it serves to promote their continued growth. Its importance is so widely recognized that many believe it to be the sole foundation upon which metropolitan integration can be built.

Throughout the country, a number of transportation studies have been organized with the avowed intention of stimulating comprehensive metropolitan planning as an offshoot of specialized transportation planning. The tristate New York City study, as well as the others, is organized, interestingly, in reflection of the realities of transportation decision making, heavily emphasizing state and federal highway-agency participation. As the Hughes Committee noted, adaptation to metropolitan transportation needs has occurred by going outside the immediate region for resources and has consequently shifted the locus of policy making for local transportation. With regard to transportation policy, New York State has taken a step just short of, or perhaps beyond, mandating local reorganization. It has assumed responsibility for the major decisions affecting the function.

PERMISSIVE LEGISLATION

Initial state action with regard to any metropolitan problem rests with the legislature. Legislative response to local requests has been a major contribution to the development of new techniques of metropolitan action. Although the legislature rarely mandates change, by passing general permissive legislation or, upon request, special legislation authorizing new forms of cooperation or joint action in one part of the state, it often initiates a process of experimentation leading eventually to significant changes in local structure and policy.

Local governments are indeed the laboratories for testing metropolitan innovations. The Onondaga County Public Works Commission's success in dealing with a multijurisdictional pollution problem is credited with inspiring the amendment to the county law enabling all counties to participate in centralized sewage-disposal programs. Today, Nassau County is similarly testing the effectiveness of a county police department. If successful, its experiment may also be incorporated into the county law.

Permissive legislation has been identified above as being either special or general. The two represent the exercise of differing degrees of legislative leadership, but their ultimate effect is much the same, as is the extent to which they condition local response. Both are dependent upon local initiative, the former prior to legislative action, the latter subsequent to it. Both offer local leaders a convenient scapegoat upon which the blame for necessary but unpopular local acts may be placed. Both eventually achieve state-wide impact through originally limited application followed by imitation and more general acceptance.

Permissive legislation can be and often is supplemented by more stimulative (forceful would not be the proper word) legislative action. A grant-in-aid may offer considerable incentive for local adoption of a new policy or form of organization. State policy toward county health units has long been at this stage of combining permissive authority and financial inducement. Given the legislature's preference for relying on local initiative and the absence of a public-health issue upon which to wage a supporting campaign, it is not likely that the legislature or the governor will act to compel local health reorganization.

STATE GRANTS-IN-AID

In recent years a number of new programs authorizing grants to counties have been enacted. Mental Health, Youth Activities, and Library grants are encouraging counties to assume more responsibilities and simultaneously are increasing the popular tendency to turn to county governments for service. Although none of these grants is offered exclusively to counties, each has been supplemented by administrative efforts to initiate county rather than town or city operations. Grant-aided activities are only a few of the impressive number that have been added to the county's auspices in recent years. Although the grant-in-aid has undoubtedly helped promote county growth, several features inherent in the use of the device seriously qualify its potential impact on metropolitan action.

There is an unmistakable local tendency to regard state grants-in-aid as a matter of right and not as a reward. The legal and historical foundations of federal and state grant programs illustrate, by comparison, the state grant's limitations as a stimulative tool. Although federal grants are increasingly coming to be regarded as existing for purposes of tax sharing and the opening of new revenue sources to smaller governmental units, the nature of the federal system still substantiates viewing federal grants as gratuitous payments, the receipt of which can be made conditional upon satisfying federal requirements and standards. In contrast, the intimate relationship of state-local finance makes it extremely difficult to impose too many conditions on the award of state grants. Indeed, the Census Bureau does not even attempt to differentiate conditional grants from shared taxes in its compilation of state payments to local governments.

When, as in public education, local programs are largely regarded as delegations of state functions, the state is under a moral obligation to dispense aid uniformly and without regard to any purposes other than the support of minimum program standards. The tendency to equate grants with shared taxes particularly inhibits the use of conditional grants in places where some state support has previously been offered. In using grants to stimulate the formation of county health units, for example, the state found it necessary to offer additional benefits to county units rather than to attempt to reduce payments to units already receiving aid for health activities. Similarly, in all its efforts to effect school centralization the legislature has never dared take the logical step of withholding grants from small districts. The grant device thus displays a great deal of inflexibility. Once offered, a grant can rarely be withdrawn, despite a change in conditions which may make it desirable to shift program emphases or organizational foundations.

The successful withdrawal of a grant appears to have been of considerable influence in promoting county assumption of one new activity. The Mental Health Act of 1956 initiated grants to county and city Mental Health Boards. Support for Child Guidance Centers were included within the new program. The Mental Health grant superseded a previous grant to Child Guidance Centers distributed by the State Youth Commission. Since the Centers had all been formerly attached to County Children's Courts or Welfare Departments, any county not forming a Mental Health Board would lose state support for its center. To several counties, anticipation of the loss of state aid was sufficient incentive to counteract objections to undertaking additional expenses for fuller mental-health programs.

In the case of mental health, the impact of a grant withdrawal was softened by the offer of substitute payments to the same unit of government. The effect would probably not be the same, for example, were the state to discontinue highway aid to towns in order to stimulate greater county highway activity. The development of highway, health, and education grants illustrate the extent to which a past stimulative grant can mold and freeze a pattern of organizational relationships. Political considerations negate the possibility of restructuring grant programs to change organizational goals.

Political realities also affect the state's ability to initiate new grants in order to redistribute existing local responsibilities. A new grant attached to a new program toward which local attitudes have not yet been set can potentially meet with more success in stimulating desired action than redesigning formulas in existing grant programs. But, in programs in operation for some time, local demands for tax relief represent a standing claim for a share of any new funds distributed by the state. It is as difficult to initiate functional redistribution by financial reward as by legislative mandate. What the legislature fears to do by mandate, it will not attempt by financial manipulation.

Tax-relief demands are today the major motivation for the state's consideration of sewage-treatment grants. The state and the federal government are under extreme pressure to provide aid to every local jurisdiction engaged in sewage disposal activities, despite professional preference for grant designs that would reward and encourage mergers and joint operations of sewage facilities. The tax-relief philosophy is one source of pressure for equal treatment. The technical objectives motivating the existing federal and the proposed state programs are a second and more fundamental pressure preventing the selective distribution of construction grants.

The foremost goal of each federal or state grant is program, rather than organizationally, oriented. As long as the purpose of health grants is to increase available health services, as long as many people regard the urban renewal program as merely the tearing down of slums and their replacement by high tax ratables, the imposition of conditions of metropolitan significance upon grant recipients are likely to be of secondary consequence. Metropolitan objectives generally coincide with program objectives, but the latter may often be satisfied by short-range action less demanding than the coordinative and redistributive ends of metropolitan integration. Grant programs tend to follow the path of least resistance.

It is impossible to ascribe a definite measure of effectiveness to any grant program. It is equally unrealistic to disregard grant impact. The grant's potential as a device for stimulating metropolitan integration has suffered from the overabundant and often conflicting ends for which the device has been used. However, even if a grant were designed solely for purposes of promoting local reorganization, its effectiveness would appear to be related to the following factors:

1. The grant must offer a financial inducement sizable enough to influence decisively the choice of local action. It must be remembered that a grant that has the effect of redistributing functions will usually result in a greater financial expenditure by one unit than has been customary in the past. Those relieved from further expenditures, i.e., the City of Buffalo, when health was transferred to Erie County, may encourage the transfer. The unit assuming new responsibilities, however, will do so only if the financial return to itself is great enough.

2. Related to the size of the grant is its time of impact. An annual grant is not as dramatic an inducement as one that is offered at a particularly crucial time for local finances. Annual aid for central school districts has not been nearly as effective as the additional aid available for the construction of new central schools.

3. A grant attached to a new program faces fewer obstacles than one relating to an ongoing local activity.

4. The activity supported by the grant must be recognized locally as a desirable and justifiable area of governmental performance. The absence of such justification, as much as the unavailability of grants, is probably responsible for the failure of counties to undertake regulatory functions. There are some things that money can't buy.

ADMINISTRATIVE SUPERVISION

One of the factors limiting the grants' usefulness in promoting metropolitan integration is their commitment to short-range goals which do not always coincide with metropolitan objectives. The functional basis upon which state executive agencies are organized imposes similar limitations on the operating values of all state officials. No state program is devoted to problems of metropolitan areas. The only state officials concerned with general local government, as opposed to individual local functions, are those dealing with the financial or legal activities of local governing bodies.[1] Their standards of review are invariably legalistic or procedural. Theirs is not to question the adequacy of local governmental organization or operation.

To the extent that the statutory authority under which they operate takes intraregional factors into account, state officials can influence and control patterns of local action, so as to maximize metropolitan objectives. This is to say something more than the frequent assertion that all state or federal activities have an impact upon metropolitan areas. It does imply that state administrative officers can promote awareness of the areal significance of some local functions, if the authority by which they act encourages and permits them to use metropolitan standards in their dealings with local officers.

State health officials today are hampered in emphasizing metropolitan health needs by legislative policies that continue to define health programs in jurisdictional terms of city, village, and town powers. The water-pollution control program, on the other hand, does more than require a certain degree of sewage treatment for each class of municipality. Its standards are based upon areal considerations of water resources. The Water Pollution Control Law contains positive stimulants to thinking in areal terms.

Increasingly, state legislative and administrative policies have called for broader thinking on the part of local units. But the emphasis on areal definitions of problems has not been accompanied by equal efforts to create metropolitan tools of action. In highway affairs the state has itself had to step in to fill a void existing between recognized need and jurisdictional

---

[1] The activities of the Office for Local Government have not yet changed the validity of this statement. Although still in the formative stage of its development, the office appears to be concentrating on serving as a clearinghouse for information of value to local governments.

capacity. In sewage treatment, the state has not yet developed a method for translating need into action. Local governments justifiably complain of their inability to conform to water classifications based upon areal factors over which they have no control. Federal stimulants to metropolitan planning in urban renewal programs are the most extreme example of the futility of injecting areal values into an operating environment lacking in capacity or willingness to deal with them. The result in both federal and state programs is the continued payment of lip service to a concept lacking a basis in operational reality.

In encouraging local governments to at least look at the broader metropolitan aspects of their programs and problems, officials in non-aided programs have a slight advantage over their colleagues in grant-aided activities. The type of local action they can suggest or encourage is not limited to the confines of a pattern of organization mandated or made more profitable by the requirements of a grant program, although, to be sure, they must remain within the limits of local choice prescribed by state, enabling legislation. Nevertheless, as evidenced by the number of permissions recently given to local governments to cooperate and join with one another in specific activities, changes in enabling legislation are more easily come by than revisions in grant formulas.

To a greater degree than their counterparts in aided programs, these state officials may vary their recommendations and the amount of pressure they exert on local officials. Thus representatives of the State Health Department and the Water Pollution Control Board could press for a metropolitan sewage-treatment solution in Onondaga County, where local factors had already created a receptive atmosphere, while accepting a different plan for pollution abatement in Broome County. The flexibility now enjoyed by these state offices may be greatly reduced by the sewage-disposal grant program now being contemplated. Its effect may be to encourage local officials to form the habit of rushing to Albany with hastily conceived plans, in order to put in early bids for available state funds.

In whatever type of program they operate, state officials bring to metropolitan problems an element of outside objectivity that is invaluable in bringing together local interests. In effect state officials act as arbiters of competing interests, bring conflicting positions out into the light, and provide the stimulus for discussion and resolution of differences. If at times the intervention of a state official serves merely to solidify resistance to a state policy, his appearance has at least had the salutory effect of evoking an expression of opinion not previously known to policy makers.

The actions of state officers have had considerable impact upon the broadening of local views. But their influence on local practices has been limited by the narrowness of their own functional orientation and by political leadership committed to the retention of existing governmental structures. Cooperation, not reorganization, is the keynote of New York's metropolitan policy—if the state can be credited with having a metropolitan policy. More accurately, New York has policies toward water pollution, subdivision control, planning, and a host of other problems *in* metropolitan areas. The state is increasingly encouraging interlocal cooperation in dealing with common problems, but, as long as adequate program standards can be obtained through individual action, state officials are compelled to accept what they may personally believe are inadequate proposals, rather than insist upon metropolitan solutions and jeopardize the possibility of any action.

THE STATE AS A METROPOLITAN AGENCY

Assuming—and this is not always true—that state officials have a broader perspective of area problems than local officials, can they not accomplish more by undertaking particular functions themselves than by attempting to stimulate metropolitan action through the limited methods of interlocal cooperation now available? Highway experience indicates that the change in relationships resulting from state assumption of an activity tends to reduce the state's ability to remain objective in acting as an arbiter of local interests. As a direct participant in metropolitan affairs, a state agency faces the choice of plunging into the process of formulating and determining the priority of local values or remaining aloof from local conflict. In effect, the state has tried to steer a middle course in its highway program; for no matter how objective they try to appear, state officials cannot help but be conscious of and try to control the impact their program has on metropolitan development.

New York State has virtually abandoned the quest, so characteristic of the 1930's, for a formula distinguishing state from local responsibilities. Today, all functions are regarded as dependent upon close state-local policy and financial relationships. Nevertheless, justification for state program operation still rests upon the assertion of a dominant state interest. In the pursuit of that interest, state policy inevitably comes into conflict with local interests. Thus, whether it chooses to or not, the state becomes embroiled in the internal conflicts of metropolitan areas.

However, the state is neither prepared nor willing to participate fully in metropolitan decision making. It is unprepared, because its concentration on single functions necessitates a particularistic, rather than general, approach to the metropolitan area and its problems. It is unwilling, because it does not wish to compromise its state-wide interest to considerations that are unrelated to the immediate results with which it is concerned. Consequently, the activity performed by the state is taken out of its local context, with an attendant disruption of program interrelationships. The state as a participant is not contributing to metropolitan integration but, instead, is eliminating one component of the metropolitan problem, without providing a mechanism for anticipating and coordinating the impact of the state program with other metropolitan issues.

The development of the federal highway program and the inability of local governments to finance large-scale highway programs have led to the state's assuming increased responsibility for metropolitan highway planning and construction. In the public-health field, particularly the health aspects of subdivision control, the state has conceded the necessity of local participation and cooperation and has sought to withdraw from the activity. Although the circumstances and motivations are not the same, by encouraging independence in local health administration and subdivision control, the State Health Department is avoiding problems similar to those arising from local reaction to state highway policies.

State officials are not local officers. Although they undoubtedly tend to reflect the attitude and interests of the area they serve, their primary responsibility is to program goals that all too often are formulated with little or no local participation, resulting in policies that are in conflict with local desires. Centralization of program control in state hands serves to increase the complexity of intergovernmental relations in metropolitan areas, not only by fragmenting responsibilities for vital governmental functions but also by adding yet another unit of government to the excessive number now participating in the governance of metropolitan areas.

THE SPECIAL DISTRICT

Although education and highways are legally and historically dissimilar, the two programs can be compared as evidence of alternative methods of state participation in local affairs. The state has supplemented existing highway activities by embarking on additional construction in areas where local authorities have their own road responsibilities. In education it has not acted as an interloper but as the unit of primary and original functional responsibility to which local officials are accountable. By having school-board members elected locally, while recognizing them as state officers, the state has been less vulnerable to charges of interference and arbitrariness and at the same time has retained formal control over the education system and its policies.

The price the state has had to pay, however, has been increasing financial support to school districts and the fostering of local loyalties that often reduce the flexibility of state control. It is often difficult to determine who is the leader and who the follower in educational administration. Over time, educational organization appears to have followed a circular rather than hierarchical principle. By means of financial incentives, the state has been able to induce a gradual geographic expansion of local districts. Slowly, and not without local opposition, the state has initiated a standard of need (pupil population), rather than a jurisdictional standard, in organizing school districts irrespective of local-government boundaries.

In effect, the school district represents a type of single-purpose special district shorn of that device's most objectionable feature—the lack of citizen participation and control. Some even suggest that the school district is the only true metropolitan government operating in New York. This assertion attributes too much significance to the school district's ability to include territories of more than one primary unit of local government. It neglects the fact that there are many more independent districts located within single towns than there are districts overlapping town, village, or city boundaries.

But the school district is still subject to the general criticism of the separatist tendencies of special districts. Even if school districts could be centralized to cover all or most of the defined limits of metropolitan areas, their continued separation from other governmental activities would still result in competitive financial policies. If anything, implementation of state policies through locally elected officials appears to make program coordination less possible than through state administration. Local election of school officials is no guarantee that educational policy will be developed with greater attention to total local needs than highway policy. State highway officials do occasionally compromise with local interests. In the enjoyment of their "unique" position, school boards have not often been known to strive for cooperation and compromise.[2]

[2] In considering the competitive position of school boards in metropolitan areas, Julius Margolis has some interesting comments, comparing the financial rewards given to independent and dependent school districts. He suggests "when a . . . function is broken out of the complex matrix of the multifunctional government and becomes institutionalized in a separate government it finds greater difficulties in maintaining levels of services because of the fiscal restraints imposed by the necessity of developing a concensus among knowledgeable voters." Commentators on his paper do not all agree with Margolis's advocacy of the package approach to politics and finance, "Metropolitan Finance Problems: Territories, Functions and Growth," in *Public Finances: Needs, Sources, and Utilization,* a report of the National Bureau of Economic Research (Princeton: Princeton University Press, 1961), pp. 229–293.

VIII

Leadership for Metropolitan Integration

The Joint Legislative Committee on Metropolitan Areas Study came to the conclusion that solutions to the problems of metropolitan areas rest eventually with local governments. Although the committee noted the need for some state action, for the most part, it regarded the state's role as facilitative and only occasionally stimulative to local innovation. The legislature has signified its general agreement with the committee's position by its actions. In effect, the state appears to be following a course long advocated by Home Rule enthusiasts, acting usually only upon the request of local authorities. Leadership for metropolitan integration in New York State rests where it probably must, at the local level.

To expect otherwise is more than unrealistic. Even though their constituencies are larger, state political leaders are subject to the same pressures that commit their local counterparts to continued metropolitan governmental fragmentation. These pressures cannot be interpreted merely in terms of self-seeking distrust on the part of politicians to any change that threatens to upset the political systems in which their interests are vested. All too often, this simple explanation is used to rationalize the defeat of proposals for metropolitan reorganization, attributing their defeat to recalcitrant politicians rather than general unpopularity. On the contrary, political opposition to reorganization suggests that democracy is in fact working. The divisions in community interest that hinder local integration are accurately reflected in the state legislature, whose members are no more nor less able to reconcile their differences than local leaders.

But are local interests adequately represented in Albany? New York has not been free from criticism on the grounds of legislative malapportionment. Is imbalanced rather than accurate representation of urban interests responsible for New York's reluctance to deal squarely with the metropolitan problem?

The positions of Long Island Republican leaders with regard both to the distribution of state aid to education in 1960 and to congressional reapportionment in 1962 would indicate that, in their eyes at least, malapportionment is less a hindrance to the achievement of their objectives than the possible consequences of a Democratic majority's being seated in the legislature. They were willing to suffer some monetary loss in compromising with rural Republicans over state aid to education rather than form a coalition with the Democratic minority. In congressional apportionment, their voices have yet to be raised in demand for deserved increases in suburban representation. They seem to prefer the present security of the Republican caucus to the instability that might result from opening wide urban-rural cleavages.[1] The Republican Party, in addition, is quite able to serve urban interests, particularly in upstate New York, where urban politics is mostly Republican politics.[2]

---

[1] David R. Derge documents the preference for party- rather than constituency-oriented legislative voting in "Metropolitan and Out-State Alignments in Illinois and Missouri Legislative Delegations," *American Political Science Review,* LII, No. 4 (December, 1958), pp. 1051–1065.

[2] The Republican Party's ability to secure intra-metropolitan cooperation in one area is a major finding of Roscoe C. Martin, Frank J.

Retaining Republican control of state policy machinery is a primary goal of upstate Republican leaders and even of some Democrats; for its alternative is Democratic control, which to many is synonomous with control of the state by New York City. This goal, in turn, is dependent upon maintaining the strength of the local roots of the Republican Party. There is then an element of self-protection in the legislature's hesitancy to tamper with local political institutions. It is operative, however, only in so far as area residents continue to believe that their limited integrative objectives are adequately being served by presently constituted political organizations. There is no evidence at this time to suggest that they feel otherwise.

Leadership is rarely expected from legislative bodies anyway. This quality is usually attributed to the Governor. Is he able to offer more positive leadership in metropolitan affairs? Those who see in the electoral basis upon which he gains office a source of strength that is denied legislators individually and collectively usually overestimate his ability to act independently of political influence and almost always place too much emphasis on the effect of legislative malapportionment. No less a leader than Governor Rockefeller has found it extremely difficult to do anything but equivocate on metropolitan policy.

In one respect, the Governor of New York is constrained from taking too strong a position on metropolitan issues even more than are other state chief executives. The shadow of the White House, so often pointed to as a factor in his favor, tempers whatever inclination he might have to chance provoking local political leaders in both New York and the nation at large. Their support is vital to his future political ambitions, particularly in New York, where nominations for key state and federal offices are decided by convention.

Munger, and others, *Decisions in Syracuse* (Bloomington: Indiana University Press), 1961.

In short, the state's political leaders are ill equipped to champion measures for far-reaching change in local governmen in the face of continuing evidence of local preference for the *status quo*. Consequently, they have adopted an attitude consistent with the Hughes Committee's belief that change will occur when local pressures for uniformity of service become undeniable.

If the political branches of state government are not providing general leadership for metropolitan integration, they are at least participating significantly in the process of adapting local governmental operations to newer problems of urbanism. At times, such participation amounts to gentle prodding and persuasion. More often it takes the form of offering municipalities the opportunity to evolve their own methods of dealing with local problems. In a sense, New York is providing a type of leadership which is, if not as vigorous as that called for by the Council of State Governments and more recently by the Advisory Commission on Intergovernmental Relations, at least more realistic.[3]

The leadership called for by the council and the commission is about as operationally definable as their concepts of the metropolitan problem. Both have taken great pains to stress their practicability, yet throughout their reports lies the suggestion that a problem more deep-rooted than that which can be solved by annexation, functional transfer, and special authority is involved in metropolitan areas. But of course, they are not recommending the formation of metropolitan governments.

New York State's position is more forthright. There is no single governmental problem in metropolitan areas, but rather

[3] In a report submitted to the House Committee on Government Operations, the Advisory Commission on Intergovernmental Relations cites favorably and comes to the same general conclusions as the Council of State Governments. *Governmental Structure, Organization, and Planning in Metropolitan Areas* (Washington: U.S. Government Printing Office, July, 1961).

a number of difficulties surrounding the provision of selected public services, which existing local institutions can continue to perform with some minor adjustments. Through different reasoning, at the same time absolving itself from the responsibility for providing leadership, New York has arrived at many of the policies advocated by the proponents of more direct state leadership : the interlocal agreement, the special authority, the encouragement of expanded county activities, and most of all the sharing of state resources with local units have typified metropolitan policy in New York State.

In the development of this policy, however, New York's leaders have consistently held to a functional outlook toward metropolitan problems and their solutions. Where general legislation has been called for to permit or encourage intermunicipal cooperation, the creation of special districts, or, as the commission put it, the building of "an 'arsenal' of remedial weapons" available to metropolitan areas, New York has preferred to deal with metropolitan problems with both geographic and functional selectivity. In one respect, it has surpassed most recommendations for dealing generally with local governments. In 1946, a per capita block grant to all local units was initiated. Critics regard this non-conditional sharing of state resources on the one hand as the best method of helping localities help themselves, on the other as the surest means of encouraging the retention of inefficient, marginal units of local government. The choice of positions is largely a matter of personal prediliction. Even were techniques of measurement available, the grant's size is as yet too small to warrant drawing any conclusions.

In pursuing its functional course, the state has virtually ignored exploring annexation as a metropolitan alternative. New York's annexation laws, in addition to the usual complexity, are extremely protective to unincorporated territories.

Considering the extent of fringe-area development that has taken place in highly urban New York since the Cornick study and the general opinion that annexation's usefulness is quite limited, its application to New York is highly questionable.

Again consistent with its over-all policy, New York has continued to extend the scope of its Home Rule law. Constitutional amendments in 1959 considerably broadened the range of county discretion and for the first time included urban towns within the scope of Home Rule. Village officials at this time were particularly apprehensive of the irresponsibility and isolationism that might thus have been encouraged. Their attitude reflects the changing light in which Home Rule has come to be viewed. At one time, it was held to be the answer to most, if not all, local ills. Today it is regarded with some misgivings. The Advisory Commission on Intergovernmental Relations seems to be echoing the early Tax Commissions' search for formulas delineating governmental responsibilities when it recommends

> local home rule for strictly local problems; metropolitan home rule for area-wide problems, but with the state free to legislate and otherwise act with respect to problems which transcend county boundaries and which are not soluble through interlocal cooperation.[4]

Conceivably, definition of the problem may become more difficult politically than its treatment!

Home Rule in New York has never served to prohibit the state from intervening, when it wanted to, in what are presumably matters of local "property, affairs, and government." The legislature and the courts have seen to that. Moreover, Home Rule has constantly been served up with conditions and procedural requirements that limit the freedom apparently offered.

The County Home Rule Amendment approved by the

---

[4] *Ibid.*, p. 20.

electorate in 1959 is illustrative of the hesitant one-step-forward, two-steps-back pace that characterizes progress in New York State. The legislature had introduced the amendment in part to formalize the considerable degree of county independence operationally developed and in part to enable counties to adjust themselves to their newer metropolitan responsibilities. It offered considerable local discretion in organizing county governments, but at the same time it restored the requirement of a double-majority approval (a majority in any city and a majority in areas outside of cities) that had been dropped from the constitution by the 1938 convention. The provision requiring a triple majority for proposed transfers of functions to counties (majorities in cities, outside areas, and all units affected by the transfer) was retained in its entirety. The Joint Legislative Committee on Metropolitan Areas Study was in the forefront of the campaign thus to aid metropolitan areas solve their problems.

FUNCTIONAL AND METROPOLITAN INTEGRATION

The interplay of local preference and state policy has resulted in the state's offering and local units' choosing forms of metropolitan action least damaging to the territorial and functional integrity of local political institutions. What has been their combined effect on metropolitan integration as previously defined?

The state must be credited with contributing to the process of metropolitan integration through fostering an awareness of areal need and encouraging local cooperation in tackling selected problems on a metropolitan scale. Departmental officials have been especially active in promoting awareness of the areal aspects of local activities. The legislature, in addition to making cooperative means of local action available, has at times taken further steps to stimulate their employment through the offer of grant inducements. While not always effective, their joint efforts have assisted in breaking down previous barriers to intermunicipal cooperation. Not to be overlooked is the fact that such cooperation has successfully reduced some of the problems of transportation, water supply, sewage disposal, public health, and others. Metropolitan areas are not falling apart at the seams.

Although the state is helping alleviate some of the most evident manifestations of the metropolitan problem and although it is contributing to integration, defined as a process involving the development of metropolitan consciousness, it has not assisted, primarily because it has not wanted to, integration conceived as the creation of institutional mechanisms for organizing and coordinating policy making in metropolitan areas. There is good reason to believe that state and local concentration on individual service problems is, in fact, hindering metropolitan integration thus defined.

Government is more than a provider of services; it is a political institution of social organization and control. As an integrative institution, government in metropolitan areas should perform the task of eliciting expressions of interest and reconciling differences. To a significant degree, the state itself is now performing this task in metropolitan areas, but none of the current service-oriented undertakings of the state or local governments appears to be contributing to the creation of local institutions for this purpose. The state's functional approach to metropolitan problems appears to be furthering additional metropolitan fragmentation along functional, rather than geographical, lines. Paradoxically, this is occuring at the very time that the county, partly as a result of state policy, is beginning to show a potential capacity to act as an integrative institution.

The cumulative effect of functional policies has been gradually to expand the scope of county responsibility and activity. A remodeled county government could well serve as the agency of metropolitan policy making and administration. Single counties presently include most of those portions of metropolitan areas experiencing the problems of urbanism. The county represents both the largest service unit and the largest unit of local self-government. It has gained in popular stature and respect with its increased responsibilities. The New York county enjoys an advantage in structure lacking in many other states that increases its attractiveness when compared with other proposals for metropolitan government. This traditional unit of government is already federally organized, although quite often disproportionately.

State policy does not, however, look toward the eventual employment of counties for metropolitan government. For the most part, the county has "just growed." Although the state has encouraged expansion of their activities, it has done so with no general scheme of development in mind. In the past, the state usually sought to limit county authority to unincorporated areas whenever possible. Although county-wide authority is today preferred for many functions, the change in attitude has been justified on administrative grounds, with little concern for the county as an institution for governing. The state's opinion of the role of counties in metropolitan-area government might well be summed up by Pope's couplet: "that which is best administered is best."

Functionalism adds a new dimension to metropolitan fragmentation. It poses a problem of integration perhaps more difficult than the mere proliferation of units of government. It fosters intracommunity divisions in interest and leadership, adding these to divisions already founded on jurisdictional lines.

Throughout the state, leadership in metropolitan areas has come to be associated with particular functions. To the extent that opportunities to exercise general leadership still exist in pluralistic American society, they are lessened by increasing isolation of functional responsibilities and horizontal division of these among several units of government. Even traditionally strong mayors have succumbed to the trend toward functional specialization and exclusiveness. They have seized upon urban renewal as their specialty, leaving other aspects of municipal leadership to other specialists and their interest groups.

Functional division of government has a dual impact on the citizen. It provides yet another obstacle to his understanding and participating in governmental decisions affecting him. Yet, it also offers him security, leading him to believe that there is really nothing wrong with local government (of this he needs little convincing) that a few more sewers or roads won't cure.

State and federal programs reinforce the functional-service definition of the metropolitan problem. They single out problems for treatment, holding out hopes that each successive project they encourage will bring an end to the metropolitan area's ills. One has only to read the glowing newspaper accounts of "how we solved our metropolitan problem" or "how our metropolitan area is progressing" that follow the announcement of new urban renewal, highway, or treatment-plant projects for visual evidence of their lulling effect. Functionalism thus tends to impede not only governmental integration but the development of metropolitan consciousness as well. When a problem has been solved there is little reason to continue to be concerned for the metropolitan area. Moreover, there is no evidence of a carry-over of metropolitan awareness from one specific problem to another.

Proponents of metropolitan action wage their campaigns within their respective fields of functional competence and rarely concern themselves with other problems, let alone with "the metropolitan problem." Each proposal for metropolitan action is considered on its own merits, with little apparent reliance on experience gained from other functional solutions, except where these have produced bitterness and resentment of "interference" and "domination." Metropolitan consciousness is as functionally oriented as metropolitan leadership.

Perhaps no amount of state activity can substitute for the local initiative necessary to progress toward metropolitan integration. Undoubtedly, metropolitan integration cannot occur until such time as the public is prepared to take a critical look at local government as a form of government, not merely as a dispenser of services. Can Albany hasten this day?

It can do so only by admitting that the metropolitan-area problem is political not administrative and that it involves the very nature of local government. It must discard the search for techniques of problem solving and concentrate on developing responsible and representative policy-making agencies in metropolitan areas. No number of functional jointures and agreements will ever provide a suitable governmental (and necessarily democratic) mechanism for planning and controlling the distribution of physical and human resources within a metropolitan area. Administration is not lacking in metropolitan areas; government is. There is little indication that New York will be prepared to adopt such a change in attitude in the foreseeable future.

Index